IN THE FOOTSTEPS OF JOSHUA

RICHARD M. DAVIDSON

REVIEW AND HERALD® PUBLISHING ASSOCIATION
HAGERSTOWN, MD 21740

This book was
Edited by Gerald Wheeler
Designed by Patricia S. Wegh
Cover design by Helcio Deslandes
Typeset: 11/12 Times

PRINTED IN U.S.A.

99 98 97 96 95   10 9 8 7 6 5 4 3 2 1

R&H Cataloging Service
Davidson, Richard M. 1945–
     In the footsteps of Joshua.

     I. Bible. O.T. Joshua—Commentaries.
I. Title.
                222.2

ISBN 0-8280-0945-7

Dedicated to

my son Jonathan—
close friend and companion in the footsteps of Joshua—
who is "entering God's rest" through baptism
as this book is being published.

Acknowledgments

Many thanks go to those who have made this book possible. My beloved wife, Jo Ann, and precious daughter Rahel—who came to love the Middle East from our previous trips but whose school responsibilities kept them from accompanying Jonathan and me this spring to Israel, where this book was sketched—have provided unfailing encouragement by letter, telephone, fax, E-mail, and courier, not to mention their constant prayers for our safety and success as well as their constructive reading of the book manuscript.

I have appreciated the some 30 seminary students and their family members who shared in our travels this spring and enthusiastically participated in the "outdoor classroom" discussions on-site in the "Promised Land."

My expert secretary, Dorothy Show, has cheerfully labored over this manuscript with efficiency and accuracy. My son Jonathan, who joined me "in the footsteps of Joshua," also has provided valuable editorial assistance.

But my greatest thanks go to the God of Joshua, who has demonstrated the same sustaining grace and power in my writing of this book as in Israel's conquest of Canaan.

Contents

Introduction

This book invites you on a journey. A journey into the world of one of the greatest leaders of all time. Into the Holy Land of the Bible. And into the drama, excitement, and adventure of God's people engaged in holy exploits for their divine Commander.

As I have studied the book of Joshua intensely over the past half-dozen years, I have become especially excited over a principle of Bible study highlighted in the last chapter of Joshua—a principle that has made the book, and the Bible as a whole, come alive for me as nothing else has done. We will explore this potent principle in depth in the final chapter of our study together, but I will describe it briefly here.

Repeatedly the Bible affirms that every Israelite in every succeeding generation after the Exodus should consider that he or she personally was a slave of Pharaoh and personally experienced the Exodus from Egypt and conquest of Canaan (see, for example, Ex. 13:8, 14-16; Deut. 5:1-4; 6:20-25; Joshua 24:6-8). Since Christians are part of spiritual Israel (Gal. 3:29), this explosive principle applies to us as well. Thus the book of Joshua is not just a history of a faraway, long-ago people, nor even the account of our spiritual roots—it is rather our personal diary, our spiritual autobiography. We are to reckon that we were there! The stories of Joshua and the conquest of Canaan happened to us. It remains for us to seek to remove our spiritual amnesia and to recapture the Joshua experience—our own experience—by every means at our disposal.

In my study of the book of Joshua, I decided to retrace the steps of Joshua and the hosts of ancient Israel. First spiritually, as I rediscovered the secrets of their success in the conquest and inheritance of the Promised Land. What happened historically in the book of Joshua, I found paralleled in my own spiritual life. I discovered the book of Joshua to be a divinely ordained blueprint for victorious Christian living, a priceless typological model for the Christian in "possessing his possessions" in Christ.

Also, I decided literally to retrace the steps of Joshua and Israel. The book of Joshua is replete with wonderful stories, momentous events, and mighty miracles that happened in real places in the Bible lands. Perhaps more than with any other biblical book, reliving Joshua's experience means visualizing where the various events took place. F. J. Bliss wrote, "If the Bible is a geographical storehouse, then this book [Joshua] is its inner chamber of jewels."[1] I longed to examine those jewels firsthand. And God opened the way.

As I write this book I find myself in the Middle East, here to walk in the footsteps of Joshua and the people of Israel as they come out of Egypt, wander in the wilderness, enter Canaan, conquer their enemies, and divide the inheritance.

This is my fifth trip to the land of Palestine, having lived here at different times for a total of about one and a half years. But during these past two months I have focused on the book of Joshua, traveling where Joshua and ancient Israel traveled, seeking to place each story and conversation in the setting where it happened. As a result, the book of Joshua has come alive in a new way for me! I would like to share some of the excitement and inspiration that have been mine while following in the footsteps of Joshua and visualizing God's mighty miracles during the Exodus from Egypt and the conquest of Canaan. The first draft of this book I wrote largely in Israel. The sentences and paragraphs in quotes without bibliographical citation I sketched on the very sites of the events described in Joshua.

The approach of this book assumes that the events described in the book of Joshua happened just as the inspired biblical writer (probably Joshua himself) recorded. Modern critical biblical scholars often deny the historicity of the Exodus and conquest narratives. They have substituted various theories for the biblical account. Some argue for a later date and a much smaller number of people for the Exodus and conquest than the Bible indicates. Others see merely successive waves of unrelated roving bands of invaders, or even a peaceful infiltration instead of any military conquest at all. And still others suggest a later organization of indigenous people into "tribes," or a sedentarization of former nomads, or a peasants' revolt within the land along the lines of Marxist ideology. The recent consensus among critical scholars is that archaeology reveals little or no trace at all of the conquest described in the book of Joshua. They see the book of Joshua as a literary fiction written centuries later than the time it purports to depict.[2]

In this book I reject the historical-critical presuppositions[3] that underlie such skeptical conclusions about the historicity of the book of Joshua. Recent reassessments of the archaeological evidence at such sites as Jericho indicate that the biblical narrative correlates well with the archaeological data.[4] Yet even if we did not have such archaeological evidence, the veracity of the Bible can stand on its own authority. We must not allow any current interpretation of what the archaeologist's spade has found to hold the Bible hostage.

As I have traced the events described in the book of Joshua, it has amazed me to see how precisely the geographical notations fit the topography of the land—so precisely that I am convinced that only an eyewitness could have written it. But I have been even more impressed by how the book of Joshua has provided supernatural power to change my own life. As I have personalized and internalized the spiritual lessons taught in Joshua, I can testify that this book is the inspired Word of God, "quick, and powerful, and sharper than any twoedged sword" (Heb. 4:12, KJV—in the context, by the way, of the story of Joshua!). I have personally experienced, and continue to experience, the spiritual and physical rest that this book records and prefigures.

The book of Joshua is not only a marvelous historically accurate narrative. And it is not only a spiritual manual for victorious living in the Christian warfare. Along with being a book of historical truth and ethical goodness, Joshua is also a book of beauty! It is beautiful in the way the author has presented his narrative in masterful literary technique. He has employed many intricate features of narrative art to powerfully portray the events described. Some of these I will note throughout this book.

Joshua is especially beautiful in its overall literary structure. The book follows a literary pattern called "panel writing" (or block parallelism), in which the second half repeats the order of the first half. God led in the events of the conquest of Canaan, recorded in the first half of the book of Joshua. He then superintended the division of the inheritance so that they would occur in a matching sequence recorded in the last half of the book. The result is a historically accurate narrative that is at the same time a literary work of beautiful symmetry. Note the following structure of the book.

Conquest	Dividing the Inheritance
A. God to Joshua: "Conquer the land" (1:1-11)	A^1. God to Joshua: "Divide and possess the land" (13:1-7)
B. Joshua to 2½ tribes (1:12-18)	B^1. Joshua to 2½ tribes (13:8-32)
C. Cross to Gilgal—Passover/ circumcision (2-5)	C^1. Gilgal—inheritance for Caleb (14:1-15)
D. Central campaign (6-8:29)	D^1. Central inheritance (15-17)
E. **Shechem**—build altar, covenant ceremony (8:30-35)	E^1. **Shiloh**—erect tabernacle, ceremony of casting lots (18:1-10)
F. Southern campaign (9-10)	F^1. Southern inheritance (18:11-19:9)
G. Northern campaign (11:1-15)	G^1. Northern inheritance (19-21)
H. Took land, land rest (11:16-23)	H^1. Gave land, rest (21:43-45)
I. Summary of conquest—area of 2½ tribes; other tribes (12)	I^1. Farewell messages—to 2½ tribes; all Israel (22-24)

We will refer to this literary structure throughout our journey in Joshua, but here we pause to note that each half of the book also has a beautiful centerpiece. The author wrote each half with the central point being the item of specific focus. It is crucial to observe in Joshua that the central focus of each half of the book is the sanctuary and its worship services! In the midst of the conquest of Canaan, before Israel's enemies were yet subdued, God commands Israel to set up an altar for worship at Shechem. Again, in the midst of the assigning of the inheritance for the 12 tribes, God directs Israel to erect the sanctuary at Shiloh for worship. The spiritual significance of these sanctuary focal points of the book will become more plain as we plunge into deeper study of Joshua's spiritual treasures.

So embark with me upon an action-packed journey! A journey of truth, goodness, and beauty. A journey through a book and through the lands of the book. A journey in the footsteps of

Joshua, toward the goal of the theme repeated most often throughout the book—entering God's rest!

---

[1] Frederick J. Bliss, *The Development of Palestinian Exploration* (New
York: Charles Scribner's Sons, 1906), p. 11.

[2] For a survey of modern critical trends and bibliography concerning the
emergence of Israel and the nature of the conquest, see William G. Dever, "Israel,
History of (Archaeology and the Israelite Conquest)," *The Anchor Bible
Dictionary* (1992), vol. 3, pp. 545-558.

[3] For a discussion of these historical-critical presuppositions, see my article
"The Authority of Scripture: A Personal Pilgrimage," *Journal of the Adventist
Theological Society,* No. 1 (1990): 39-56. See also Gerhard F. Hasel, *Biblical
Interpretation Today* (Washington, D.C.: Biblical Research Institute, 1985);
Gerhard Maier, *The End of the Historical-Critical Method* (St. Louis: Concordia,
1977); and Eta Linnemann, *Historical Criticism of the Bible* (Grand Rapids:
Baker, 1990).

[4] See chapter 6 for discussion and bibliography.

Joshua, God's Man

1

Sunday, April 17, 1994, 2:16 p.m. We are now at the probable location of Israel's crossing of the Red Sea. It fits all the geographical data described in Scripture and the Spirit of Prophecy.[1] A camp 'beside the sea, whose waters presented a seemingly impassable barrier before them, while on the south a rugged mountain obstructed their further progress' (*Patriarchs and Prophets*, pp. 283, 284; cf. Ex. 14:2, 3). Just below the modern town of Suez and the northern tip of the Gulf of Suez is the only place in northern Egypt where a mountain (Jebel' Ataqa) comes right down to the Red Sea and blocks further passage south.

"As we drive along the eastern edge of the Gulf of Suez, just opposite to where the mountain plunges down to the sea on the western shore, I imagine Joshua and the rest of Israel's mighty host at this spot singing the Song of Moses. I cannot help lifting up my voice in the taxi and singing the mighty words of that sublime song sung by ancient Israel and that will be sung again by the redeemed on the sea of glass:

" 'I will sing unto the Lord, for he hath triumphed gloriously: the horse and his rider hath he thrown into the sea' (Ex. 15:1, KJV; cf. Rev. 15:3)."

The route of the Exodus along the shore of the Red Sea, through the Wilderness of Shur, has been vividly described by one who may well have viewed the scene in vision—"bare, desolate-looking mountains, barren plains, and the sea stretching far away, its shores strewn with the bodies of their enemies" (*Patriarchs and*

Prophets, p. 291). Southward Israel journeys, past the oases and camping places of Marah (Ex. 15:23-26; probably ᶜAin Hawârah, about 47 miles southeast of the modern city of Suez and seven miles east of the Red Sea) and Elim (verse 27; probably on the Wâdî Gharandel, about 60 miles southeast of Suez).

The wide, flat, desolate expanse of the Shur Wilderness offers plenty of room for the more than 2 million people who came out of Egypt. But shortly after Elim, the route toward Mount Sinai turns eastward and appears to be blocked by the rugged ranges of mountains in the central Sinai Peninsula. Perhaps Joshua, Israel's general, never having traveled this way before, wondered how so many people would penetrate through the mountainous barrier.

This concern had often crossed my mind as I read the Exodus account. But following in the footsteps of Joshua and Israel clears up the apparent difficulty. For as one travels toward the majestic mountain range, there suddenly appears, seemingly out of nowhere, a mighty valley (actually a wadi, or dry riverbed, called Wâdî Feirân) that winds its way east through the mountains.[2] Like a highway in the mountainous desert, it resembles from the air a huge white glacier flowing through the Sinai Peninsula. It is more than a half-mile wide, flat, smooth, with a stream bed on one side and massive granite and limestone peaks on either side—plenty of room for Israel to camp, stretched out along the wide expanse of the wadi.

Joshua the General

About two thirds of the way up Wâdî Feirân, and still some 25 miles northwest of Mount Sinai, Israel camps at Rephidim, the modern Feirân oasis. "I look out at thick groves of palm trees and lush gardens stretching across the wadi for several miles. I look up at Jebel Serbâl and Jebel Banât, rearing their lofty summits on either side of the oasis. Here I relive hearing the complaints of the people for water. I can understand their distress since I'm passing through at the very time Israel took this route, in the late spring between Passover and Pentecost, and the desert is already hot and dry! It's stifling in the taxi, until a cloud passes overhead and gives us some relief—and I imagine the cooling shade of the pillar of cloud supplied by God.

"I visualize Moses obeying God's command and striking a rock on the mountain beside the camp, and water gushing out of the mountain, down the riverbed for miles for the hosts of Israel to come to the living stream and drink."

At Rephidim we get our first glimpse, the first biblical mention, of Joshua—the brilliant general (see Ex. 17:8-16). If Israel had been trusting fully in God, they never would have had to fight, for the Lord would have prevented their enemies from attacking, or would have delivered His people miraculously as at the Red Sea. But because of Israel's complaints against Him, God allowed the fierce, warring tribe of the Amalekites, who lived in the region, to attack them.

Rising some 700 feet above the Feirân oasis is a hill on which, according to tradition, Moses stood with Aaron and Hur, watching the battle against the attacking Amalekites. As we passed through the oasis, I relived in my imagination the movements of the battle, Israel prevailing as long as Moses' arms remained upraised, and the enemy having the ascendancy when Moses lowered them. The battle teaches a beautiful lesson. Joshua put forth all possible human effort, but the real success came as a result of reaching toward heaven for divine help.

What kind of man was Joshua the general? Ellen White describes his character qualities some 40 years later as he stood on the borders of Canaan:

"Joshua was now the acknowledged leader of Israel. He had been known chiefly as a warrior, and his gifts and virtues were especially valuable at this stage in the history of his people. Courageous, resolute, and persevering, prompt, incorruptible, unmindful of selfish interests in his care for those committed to his charge, and, above all, inspired by a living faith in God—such was the character of the man divinely chosen to conduct the armies of Israel in their entrance upon the Promised Land" (*Patriarchs and Prophets*, p. 481).

Joshua the Prime Minister

Israel continued from Rephidim a little farther up the Wâdi Feirân, and then came through one of the "deep, gravelly passes. . . . Between the rocky cliffs rising hundreds of feet on either side flowed in a living tide, far as the eye could reach, the hosts of Israel with their flocks and herds. And now before them in solemn majesty Mount Sinai lifted its massive front" (*ibid.*, p. 301).

God's people set up their camp on the smooth, flat sandy plain (called er-Râḥah) in front of the northwest spur of Mount Sinai (named Ras eṣ-Ṣafṣafeh). The plain of er-Râḥah, the only plain suitable for an encampment around Mount Sinai, is at least a mile wide and two miles long, providing sufficient space for Israel to have pitched their tents in a hollow square that left room for the sanctuary in their midst.[3]

It is astounding to realize, upon reading the account of Exodus 19-24 closely, that the 80-year-old Moses ascended Mount Sinai some *six* times in the space of a few days![4] Our group of seminary students climbed and stayed on top of Mount Sinai all Friday night. I preached the Sabbath sermon at the summit on the topic of Moses' many ascents. We all agreed that our weariness from our one ascent of Jebel Mûsā made us appreciate Moses' physical vigor.

And also that of Joshua. For on the sixth ascent Moses came up the mountain with him (Ex. 24:13). As I read the account of that occasion from the top of Jebel Mûsā, the pieces of the puzzle began to fit together. Jebel Mûsā (Mountain of Moses), reaching 7,497 feet in elevation, is the highest point of the two-peaked granite mountain mass rising south of er-Râḥah plain. Its summit is the southeastern peak of the mountain and not visible from the plain. The peak to the northwest, Ras eṣ-Ṣafṣafeh (Mountain of the Willow, 6,542 feet), towers directly above the plain and is probably "the top of the mount" (Ex. 19:20), where God appeared in dazzling majesty to the people of Israel camped directly below. Surmounting Ras eṣ-Ṣafṣafeh is a forbidding, trailless rock climb for experienced climbers only. (Moses never climbed this peak in the narrative.) Some of our group managed to reach the summit, and from there we had a breathtakingly spectacular view of the plain. I imagined the thousands of tents pitched neatly by tribe, and God's ineffable glory engulfing the peak.

In the saddle between the two peaks of Mount Sinai (Jebel Mûsā and Ras eṣ-Ṣafṣafeh) is a lower basin whose granite composition collects the scant rainwater and forms a small lake of water. As I reconstructed the events in my sermon from the top of

Jebel Mûsā looking down onto the basin cradled between us and Ras eṣ-Ṣafṣafeh in the distance, I described how Moses and Joshua came together "up on the mountain" (Ex. 24:13, NIV), probably as far as the lower basin, which has some tree shade and a water source. Here Moses left Joshua, as God summoned him on Sabbath to come farther "up into the mountain" (verses 15, 16), to the top of Jebel Mûsā. While Moses was with God receiving instructions for the construction of the sanctuary, Joshua probably remained in the lower saddle between Jebel Mûs and Ras eṣ-Ṣafṣafeh, where he could eat and drink.

After the 40 days, when Moses returned to Joshua and they began their descent from the saddle around Ras eṣ-Ṣafṣafeh (perhaps down by the present St. Catherine's Monastery), they were still not able to see the plain. But Joshua heard the shouts filtering up from the plain, and with his soldier mentality, said to Moses: "There is a noise of war in the camp" (Ex. 32:17). Moses knew better, and as they rounded the last bend at the foot of Ras eṣ-Ṣafṣafeh, they saw the people dancing before the golden calf.

The story of the golden calf and its aftermath is familiar to most, yet often in the telling Joshua gets left out. Note the position of trust Moses committed to him. Moses placed his own tent outside the camp to function as the tabernacle of meeting where he communed with God. Whereas Moses would return to the camp to carry out his duties during the day, "his servant [minister] Joshua the son of Nun, a young man, did not depart from the tabernacle" (Ex. 33:11).

During his young manhood Joshua was already trustworthy and entrusted with high honor as Moses' "minister." The modern English equivalent of the Hebrew word *mešârēṯ*, used to describe Joshua's office, is "minister," or better, "prime minister." The Hebrew word implies service, but in the sense of "ministerial service," in contrast to another Hebrew word ᶜ*ebed*, which often implies "menial service." It is ironic but very instructive that Scripture often describes Moses as the Lord's menial servant (ᶜ*ebed*), while it depicts Joshua as Moses' prime-minister (*mešârēṯ*). In the final chapter of the book of Joshua, however, describing his death, the text also calls him the Lord's ᶜ*ebed*, or menial servant.

17

Joshua the Faithful Scout

The next glimpse we get of Joshua is in his role of faithful scout. One does not realize how rugged the land through which the 12 spies passed and how far they traveled until one drives the expanse of bleak and wild desert between Kadesh-barnea and the first settlements in Israel on the edge of the Negeb, and then up to the very northern borders of modern Israel. The Bible records that the spies went north from the wilderness of Paran, following Moses' instruction: "Go up this way into the South [Negeb], and go up to the mountains" (Num. 13:17). The spies scouted from the wilderness of Zin in the south to even beyond the northern border of modern Israel, "as far as Rehob, near the entrance of Hamath" (verse 21), in the Orontes Valley of modern Syria, a total journey of about 250 miles in either direction!

The Numbers account focuses especially upon their experience on the heights of the hill country in the vicinity of the Canaanite city of Hebron, where the giants descended from Anak lived.

"Thursday, May 26. This is the last day of our study program for the spring of 1994. Day after tomorrow I leave for the U.S.A. I have delayed going to Hebron because I hear that it is really not safe for tourists to visit. Only a few weeks ago dozens of Arab worshipers were gunned down by a deranged Israeli physician at the sacred Muslim enclosure over the ancient Cave of Machpelah. Hebron is the hotbed of clashes between Arab and Israeli fanatics and terrorists, and thus has been off-limits to regular tourists for several years. Now, after the Hebron massacre, the holy places are closed to all, and heavily armed Israeli soldiers guard the city.

"But I am impelled to go. In my stay this spring in the Middle East, I have revisited all the major sites connected with Joshua's life—except Hebron . . .

"I am traveling on an Arab bus to Hebron. My two student companions and I are the only Americans on the bus. We are now passing through the Valley of Eshcol, just north of Hebron. On both sides of the road grow luxurious grape vineyards, filling the valley with verdure and beauty. The Arab businessman sitting next to me, a native of a nearby village, proudly proclaims that this valley grows the biggest and best grapes in Palestine and the world.

"My mind wanders to my first visit to Israel in 1967, just one week after the Six-Day War, when I came to the Valley of Eshcol at the season of the first-ripe grape harvest (midsummer), the same time as the spies had arrived. I had read the biblical account of the gigantic clusters of grapes that the spies found in the Valley of Eshcol, but was sure that it must be partial hyperbole. However, my eyes bulged in amazement as I looked at the biggest grapes I had ever seen in my life—each grape the size of a Michigan purple plum, each cluster so heavy that it was difficult to lift with one hand. The Valley of Eshcol is still a land of bounteous harvests . . .

"And Hebron is still a city of danger. I am jolted back to the present as the Arab bus arrives in downtown Hebron, and we begin to walk through the city. It is unnerving. All the shops are closed. We are the only tourists in town. Soldiers appear at every intersection with roadblocks or checkpoints. I have a lump in my throat. My heart is beating faster. The few Arabs in the streets look at us apprehensively, and we wave and greet them all with a nervous 'Assalamu ᶜalaykum.' Militant Jewish settlers walk past us carrying automatic weapons, each with a finger on the trigger, and we greet them also, with a trying-to-be-brave 'Shalom.'

"As we near the massive Herodian-built boundary wall of the shrine over the Cave of Machpelah, soldiers, surprised to see tourists in the city, wave us back. We persuade them in halting Hebrew that we are just going to take pictures, and they finally allow us to enter the grounds. But other soldiers soon approach and insist that we must leave.

"As we walk back through the city, one Jewish member of the Peace Now group stops to talk. 'Welcome to sad city,' he says. An Arab shopkeeper asks, 'What are you doing here? Are you reporters?' When we assure him that we are American tourists, he relaxes and invites us for tea. He shows us the bruises from beatings and the scars from bullet wounds in the leg and side that he has received in the recent demonstrations. We meet white-clad members of the TIPH (Temporary International Presence in Hebron) and talk to a representative from Norway. None of them are carrying weapons. One of them tells us, 'There are enough weapons in Hebron already.' . . .

"Now on the way back from Hebron, again through the vineyards of Eshcol in an Arab taxi with one fellow 'spy' from the

19

U.S.A. and five Arab passengers, I think of Caleb and Joshua returning to camp with the fruits of the land. I imagine what they were thinking—the beautiful fruits of Eshcol and exquisite setting of Hebron on the heights of the central hill country of Canaan. What a beautiful place! But how fraught with danger. How impossible, humanly speaking, to take the city, to conquer the giants.

"The massive and seemingly impregnable stone walls of the Herodian structure in Hebron remind me of the impregnability of the whole city of Hebron at the time of the 12 spies. I think of the faith of the two spies and of the courage of Caleb, who later said to Joshua, 'Give me this mountain,' and conquered Hebron in the strength of the Lord. I determine anew to be a faithful representative of God, willing to go forward on God's missions, pressing the conquest wherever He may lead."

Even though I returned from Hebron to discover that someone had stolen my camera so that I have no pictures as "fruits" of the land—yet the memory of that visit will forever remain indelibly etched upon my mind.

Ellen White powerfully portrays the contrast of character between the 10 unfaithful spies on one hand, and Caleb and Joshua on the other:

"Hope and courage gave place to cowardly despair, as the spies uttered the sentiments of their unbelieving hearts, which were filled with discouragement prompted by Satan. . . . Caleb comprehended the situation, and, *bold to stand in defense of the word of God*, he did all in his power to counteract the evil influence of his unfaithful associates. . . .

"But the ten, interrupting him, pictured the obstacles in darker colors than at first. . . . These men, having entered upon a wrong course, stubbornly set themselves against Caleb and Joshua, against Moses, and against God. Every advance step rendered them the more determined. They were resolved to discourage all effort to gain possession of Canaan. They distorted the truth in order to sustain their baleful influence" (*Patriarchs and Prophets*, pp. 388, 389; italics supplied).

The history of the 12 spies repeats itself today.

"The scenes of cowardly complaining and drawing back from action when there are risks to be encountered are reenacted among us today. The same unwillingness is manifested to heed the faithful reports and true counsel as in the days of Caleb and Joshua. The servants of God, who bear the burden of His cause, practicing strict self-denial and suffering privation for the sake of helping His people, are seldom better appreciated now than they were then. . . . The church needs faithful Calebs and Joshuas who are ready to accept eternal life on God's simple condition of obedience" *(Testimonies,* vol. 4, pp. 154-156).

Joshua the Successor of Moses

After Israel's rebellion against the Lord at Kadesh-barnea, following the lead of the 10 unfaithful spies, God consigns all the adults except Caleb and Joshua to die in the wilderness.

Forty years in the wilderness pass. God finally instructs Israel to head for Canaan. I have the privilege of traversing the same territory that the Israelites passed through and experience the dramatic change in climate as the road rises from the hot desert to a "vast, elevated plain, swept by cool, fresh breezes" *(Patriarchs and Prophets,* p. 433). In contrast to the barren wasteland, we see the "green spots among the hills and valleys of Edom" *(ibid.,* p. 424). We ourselves take the King's Highway, denied to Israel by the king of Edom. From the height of Sela ("the rock," probably the biblical capital of the Edomites, a strenuous mountaineering route four of us took to the top) we see Mount Hor raising its lofty peak in the distance and imagine Aaron dying in Moses' arms at the summit (Num. 33:37-39; see *Patriarchs and Prophets,* pp. 426, 427). Together we visualize Israel traveling around Edom, and like them we cross the deep gorges of the Brook Zered and the Arnon River. One can imagine Joshua leading Israel to a glorious victory over the Amorite king of Heshbon. After visiting the site of Tel-el-Umeiri, which may prove to be biblical Heshbon, from the height of Mount Nebo we look down to the Plains of Moab, northeast of the Dead Sea, on the eastern bank of the Jordan River (see Num. 26:3).

Here in the Plains of Moab, amid the acacia groves by the Jordan River, God tells Moses to anoint Joshua as his successor. As he does so, the Lord explicitly mentions Joshua's crucial qualifying characteristic: "Take Joshua the son of Nun with you, a man in whom is the Spirit, and lay your hand on him" (Num. 27:18).

This same quality of being filled with the Holy Spirit distinguishes other Old Testament leaders (see Ex. 31:3; Judges 3:10; 6:34; 11:29; Ps. 51:11, 12; Eze. 2:2; Dan. 4:18; 5:14). And the Holy Spirit, just as essential for spiritual leadership today, is available to all who are willing to receive:

"In the great and measureless gift of the Holy Spirit are contained all of heaven's resources. It is not because of any restriction on the part of God that the riches of His grace do not flow earthward to men. If all were willing to receive, all would become filled with His Spirit" (*Christ's Object Lessons*, p. 419).

Moses ordains Joshua for service by the laying on of hands: "Joshua had long attended Moses; and being a man of wisdom, ability, and faith, he was chosen to succeed him. Through the laying on of hands by Moses, accompanied by a most impressive charge, Joshua was solemnly set apart as the leader of Israel" (*Patriarchs and Prophets*, pp. 462, 463). His ordination becomes a paradigm, or model, for the practice of ordination in the early Christian church and for today. Any study of the theology of ordination must begin with the profound insights contained in the account of Joshua's experience.[5]

"Wednesday, April 13. I am on top of Mount Nebo as I write these lines. We have taken the same route as Moses from the plains of Moab by the River Jordan where it enters the Dead Sea, some 1,300 feet below sea level, ascending up into the Abarim range of mountains (known in the Bible as Mount Pisgah) to one of its loftiest summits, Mount Nebo, almost 4,000 feet above the plains below. On the way I see the hillsides green with ripening crops of grain and spring grass dotted with wildflowers of brilliant hues—red, blue, and yellow. I imagine Moses making his way slowly up the steep ascent also in the springtime, and through his eyes I look out over the Promised Land.

"It is a clear day, and one can see the Dead Sea as far south as En-Gedi, to the west the plain of Jericho, the barren slopes of the Judean wilderness, with the Mount of Olives visible on the western skyline; to the north, Mount Gerizim and Mount Ebal, the mountains of Gilboa and Mount Tabor, the land of Gilead, and even the snow-covered peak of Mount Hermon. It is a glorious Promised Land!

"I imagine Moses, after his vision of the Promised Land, laid to rest and buried by the Lord, later to rise and ascend to the heavenly Canaan.

"And then I look down once more on the acacia groves below me, where Joshua and the children of Israel camped as the drama of the book of Joshua begins. Before me is the stage on which occur the adventures described in this action-packed book."

During the first stage of our journey in the footsteps of Joshua we have traveled from Egypt to Canaan, stopping at Rephidim, Sinai, Hebron, and the plains of Moab. Now we see Joshua, wise general, loyal prime minister, faithful scout, and Spirit-filled leader, poised, ready to lead the hosts of Israel into God's rest in the land "filled with milk and honey."

---

[1] My suggestions for the geographical backdrop of the Exodus and wilderness wanderings of Israel are in basic harmony with that presented in the *Seventh-day Adventist Bible Commentary* and *Seventh-day Adventist Bible Dictionary,* but I take responsibility for, and certainly am not dogmatic about, the fine points that I have concluded after personal observation of the territory over which Israel traversed, and after my own reading of the biblical text and commentary of Ellen White.

[2] Ellen White must have had this place in mind as she wrote: "Often as they had traversed the sandy wastes, they had seen before them rugged mountains, like huge bulwarks, piled up directly across their course, and seeming to forbid all further progress. But as they approached, openings here and there appeared in the mountain wall, and beyond, another plain opened to view" *(Patriarchs and Prophets,* p. 301).

[3] I calculated the space needed for a modern bedouin tent, with sufficient surrounding living space, and multiplied by an approximate number of families representing 600,000 men, and found the plain of er-Râhah sufficient to sustain this size of group, with the several wadis and smaller plains branching off from the main er-Râhah providing room for the flocks and herds and the encampments of the mixed multitude. On all sides of the plain are mountains, the foothills of which would provide areas for the sanitary waste. I walked the full length and breadth of the plain, and grew excited to see how this plain—the only plain of such size and suitability for camping in the environs of Mount Sinai—fits the biblical narrative.

[4] See Ex. 19:3, 8, 20; 20:21; 24:1, 12. He also ascended another two times some days later, as recorded in Ex. 32:30; 34:2.

[5] A dissertation presently in progress at Andrews University Theological Seminary by Keith Mattingly is examining in detail the passages dealing with Joshua's ordination.

The
Two Joshuas

2

Joshua is a type of Christ. The book of Joshua presents the divinely ordained typology of victorious Christian living.

Types . . . typology.

Whenever I mention the subject of typology in my classes or sermons, I get one of several responses. Some say, "Typology—oh, no!" They consider it to be a fanciful allegorical approach to Scripture that is subjective and without controls. Others say, "Typology—wow and amen!" Excited about studying the gospel in the types of Scripture, they cannot get enough typological material. And others say, "Typology—what's that?" They have no clear idea what the word means.

I have personally had all three reactions in my own life experience. As a theology student in college, I had a religion teacher who sought to discredit the Old Testament types as genuine foreshadowings of Christ and the gospel. For several years I as a young pastor accepted his skeptical attitude toward the Old Testament and wanted nothing to do with any fanciful allegorical approaches to Scripture. Then the beauty of the gospel dawned upon my consciousness in a new way, and at the same time the authority of the Bible took control of my life again. Studying the Old Testament with fresh perspective, I became convinced anew that the Old Testament beautifully presents the gospel largely through its typology. Eagerly I sought everything I could find that dealt with typology.

But at this point a new problem arose, a problem concerning

the nature and proper interpretation of typology. The different authors that I read seemed to come up with their own lists of types, and their own interpretation of what the types meant. None of them agreed with one another, and many of their interpretations seemed to rest on tenuous speculations rather than sound principles and controls set forth in Scripture itself. I began to wonder, What is the true basis of biblical typology, after all? This weighty question eventually drove me back to school for doctoral studies and emerged as the topic of my dissertation.

What Is Typology?

In my doctoral research I found even more scholarly disagreement about the nature, function, and purpose of typology. I discovered that although many had asserted what constituted typology, no one had really wrestled with the fundamental questions, examining the biblical basis of the typological relationships in Scripture.

For many months I struggled to find a key from within Scripture itself that would unlock this conundrum about the nature of typology. Every discussion that I read basically assumed the definition of typology without letting its basic contours emerge from the inspired text.

At last, as I agonized with God one night in a particularly meaningful prayer session for divine illumination, the light dawned upon my consciousness. I felt impressed that the word "type" was the key. This word is found in Greek *(typos)* as well as English, and a number of times Scripture uses it in a technical sense to designate the New Testament writers' interpretations of the Old Testament. At last a terminological control! Where the biblical writer chooses the word "type" (Greek *typos*) as a technical term to designate what he is interpreting, there certainly is typology. By a careful analysis of these passages, I concluded that the basic elements of typology should emerge from within Scripture without imposing a definition from outside.

A number of passages in the New Testament are clearly typological because they use the word "type" (Greek *typos*) or "antitype" (Greek *antitypos*, "corresponding to the type") in a technical sense to describe the writer's interpretation of the Old Testament: Romans 5:14; 1 Corinthians 10:6, 11; Hebrews 8:5; 9:24; and

1 Peter 3:21. As I did a detailed study of the verses in their larger contexts,[1] it excited me to observe the beautiful harmony among the different New Testament authors and the consistent picture of typology that I found emerging.

It became clear that the traditional understanding of typology—utilized by Seventh-day Adventists especially in their study of the sanctuary—stood confirmed by Scripture. Typology is the study of persons, events, or institutions (the types) that God has divinely designed to prefigure their end-time fulfillments (the antitypes) in Christ and in the gospel realities brought about by Him.

Identifying the Biblical Types: Old Testament Controls

One of the most rewarding results of this study was the realization that the New Testament writers do not arbitrarily read a typological meaning back into the Old Testament, as many have often claimed. If they did this, typology would be an illegitimate eisegesis—reading into Scripture what is not really there. But New Testament writers insist that certain persons, events, and institutions were *divinely designed from the outset* to serve as predictive prefigurations.

It was thrilling to learn that the Old Testament types referred to by the New Testament writers had already been identified as typological before the antitypical fulfillment. In the Old Testament scriptures, God has pointed out before the time of fulfillment which persons, events, or institutions are typological, and Jesus and the New Testament writers simply announce what He has already divinely indicated in advance. I had found the "missing link" that I had been looking for in typology—an inner biblical control identifying the types.

Thus with regard to persons—for example, Moses is a type of Christ, and Moses himself reveals this in Deuteronomy 18:15-19. The New Testament writers announce the fulfillment of his divinely inspired words (see John 1:21; 6:14; 7:40). Again, Elijah is a type of the new Elijah who would be the forerunner of Christ, and we notice this indicated already in the Old Testament in Malachi 4:5, 6.

As for regard to events, we see, for example, that the account of Israel's exodus from Egypt is typological because already in the

Old Testament we observe numerous verbal prophetic indicators that the Messiah would come in the context of a new Exodus, recapitulating in His life the experience of ancient Israel in their Exodus, going over the same spiritual ground but succeeding where they had failed (see, for example, Isa. 11:15, 16; 35; 40:3-5; 41:17-20; 42:14-16; 43:1-3, 14-21; 48:20, 21; 49:8-12; 51:9-11; 52:3-6, 11, 12; 55:12, 13; Jer. 16:14, 15; 23:4-8; Hosea 2:14, 15; 11:1; 12:9, 13; 13:4, 5).

And with institutions we find, for example, that the Israelite sanctuary, from the very first instructions for its construction, has an accompanying indication that it is a typological copy of the heavenly original (Ex. 25:9, 40; see also Ps. 11:4; 18:6; 60:6; 63:2; 68:35; 96:6; 102:19; 150:1; Isa. 6; Jonah 2:7; Micah 1:2; Hab. 2:20; etc.).

The Old Testament controls for typology, with illustrations, I have summarized in the following chart:

Identifying Biblical Types: Old Testament Controls

Old Testament Type (Person/ Event/Institution)	Old Testament Verbal Indicator of Typology	New Testament Announcement of Antitype
1. Exodus Exodus; Hosea 11:1	**New Exodus** Hosea 2:14, 15; 12:9, 13; 13:4-5; Jer. 23:4-8; 16:14, 15; 31:32; Isa. 11:15, 16; 35; 40:3-5; 41:17-20; 42:14-16; 43:1-3, 14-21; 48:20, 21; 49:8-12; 51:9-11; 52:3-6, 11, 12; 55:12, 13	**Antitypical Exodus** Matt. 1-5; Luke 9:31
2. Sanctuary Ex. 25-40	**Heavenly Original** Ex. 25:40; Ps. 11:4; 18:6; 60:6; 63:2; 68:35; 96:6; 102:19; 150:1; Isa. 6; Jonah 2:7; Micah 1:2; Hab. 2:20	**Heavenly Original** Heb. 8:5; 9:24; Rev. 8:1-5; 11:19; 16:1
3. David Psalms (for example, Ps. 22)	**New David** Jer. 23:5; Eze. 34:23; 37:24; Isa. 9:5, 6; 11:1-5; Hosea 3:5; Amos 9:11; Zech. 8:3	**Antitypical David** John 19:24

Old Testament Type (Person/ Event/Institution)	Old Testament Verbal Indicator of Typology	New Testament Announcement of Antitype
4. Elijah 1 Kings 17-19	**New Elijah** Mal. 4:5, 6	**Antitypical Elijah** Matt. 11:14; Mark 9:11; Luke 1:17
5. Moses Pentateuch	**New Moses** Deut. 18:15-19	**Antitypical Moses** John 1:21; 6:14; 7:40

Joshua Typology: What's in a Name?

Now, with this background on biblical typology in mind, we can ask, What biblical evidence is there—especially in the Old Testament—that God truly intended Joshua to be a type of Jesus?

It already appears in Joshua's name! Originally he was named Hoshea, meaning "salvation." But in Numbers 13:16 we find that Moses, apparently under God's direction, changed it to Joshua: "the Lord [Yahweh] is salvation." A divine change of name in Scripture is a call to look more closely at the meaning of the name, and the character and mission that the changed name reveals. We find this true already with Abram/Abraham (Gen. 17:1-8), Sarai/Sarah (verses 15-19), and Jacob/Israel (Gen. 32:22-32).

The name Joshua is a departure from all other names appearing thus far in Scripture. Look all through the Pentateuch, including Genesis, Exodus, Leviticus, and the first half of Numbers. You will find no name like it up to his time (although many similar names come later in the biblical record). It is the first theophoric name in the Bible—that is, the first record of the divine name (Yahweh) becoming part of a human name. Thus it seems to be no accident that God gave this divine-human kind of name first to Joshua as a hint of the special mission of the one (or One) bearing this name in uniting humanity and God. The name highlights the "Immanuel principle"—God with us!

With our English distinction between the names *Joshua* and *Jesus,* it is difficult for the full force of Joshua's name to sink in. But in Hebrew and Greek, Joshua and Jesus are one and the same.

Joshua bears the very name of the Messiah! It does not appear co-incidental that God inspired Moses to give to Joshua the very name reserved from all eternity for the coming Messiah.

One Hebrew scholar, Saul Levin, argues that the name of Joshua's father further underscores the unusual and special significance of Joshua's mission.[2] The Hebrew Bible indicates that Joshua was the son of Nun (Ex. 33:11; Num. 13:8, 16; Deut. 32:44; 34:9; 1 Chron. 7:27). In late (Mishnaic) Hebrew, Nun can mean "fish," but the Hebrew Bible never uses it with this meaning. Nun is also the fourteenth letter of the Hebrew alphabet and thus here could be spelling out the letter N. It would then be an evasive patronymic expression, "Joshua the son of N." The Hebrew Bible may signal this latter possibility by employing an unusual form of the word "son" *(bin*, not the usual *ben)*. The Greek translation of the name of Joshua's father is not Nun, but *naue*, which Levin argues is an Aramism for the divine name Yahweh. Thus the Bible could be introducing Joshua as "son of Yahweh"! If this is correct, it further denotes Joshua's special relation to the Lord and hints at the typological connection with the Messiah, God's Son. While Levin's arguments are not beyond question, they are certainly intriguing possibilities.

The Pentateuch also dramatically introduces the unique character of Joshua's connection with the mission of the Son of God by comparing the work God assigned to Joshua with that of the preexistent Christ, the "Angel of the Lord." The descriptions of Joshua's mission and that of the Angel of the Lord contain numerous parallel expressions, using exactly the same Hebrew words. Both Joshua and the Angel of the Lord were to "cross over before" and "go before" Israel and "bring them into the land" and "cause them to inherit" it (cf. Ex. 23:23; Num. 27:17, 21; Deut. 3:28; 31:3, 23). The comparisons are clear in their message: Joshua is doing the same work as the Angel of the Lord!

With such close parallels in the mission of Joshua and the divine Angel, Christ, it seems important to note that the Lord says, regarding the Angel: "My name is in Him" (Ex. 23:21). Joshua bears the first recorded theophoric name, and the Angel has the divine name in Himself. Thus the name of the Messiah is connected with the person of Joshua.

What Scripture hints at with regard to the name of the first Joshua becomes more explicit with regard to the post-Exilic Joshua mentioned by the prophet Zechariah. The word of the Lord came to Zechariah, saying, "Then speak to him [Joshua], saying, 'Thus says the Lord of hosts, saying, "Behold, the Man whose name is the BRANCH!"'" (Zech. 6:12). The prophet equates the name of Joshua with the Messiah, the Branch. Already the Old Testament identifies the name of the coming Messiah as Joshua— Jesus! And the deliberate identity of name and mission also indicates that the Old Testament Joshua is a type of the New Testament Joshua, the Messiah.

Joshua the Second Moses

The Pentateuch gives a further prophetic indicator that Joshua is a type of Christ in the predictive statements Moses made in Deuteronomy 18. Moses tells the people of Israel before His death that "the Lord your God will raise up for you a Prophet like me from your midst, from your brethren. Him you shall hear" (verse 15). Israel's leader then says that the Lord Himself had given this prediction: "I will raise up for them a Prophet like you from among their brethren, and will put My words in His mouth, and He shall speak to them all that I command Him" (verse 18).

From reading the parallels between the work of Moses and that of Joshua his successor (see, for example, Joshua 1:2-5; 3:7; 4:14), it would seem natural to expect that he was the predicted prophet like unto Moses. However, the final verses of Deuteronomy—which the text itself indicates was added under inspiration later, very possibly by Ezra toward the end of Old Testament history[3]—make clear that although Joshua was indeed Moses' successor, he was not in the fullest sense that Prophet like Moses who was to arise. For "since then there has not arisen in Israel a prophet like Moses, whom the Lord knew face to face" (Deut. 34:10).

The implication is that while Joshua partially fulfilled the prediction, the ultimate antitypical fulfillment still remained in the future—in the person of Jesus the Messiah. Thus Joshua's life, like Moses', typologically foreshadowed the coming Messiah. This is parallel to the prophecy of Isaiah 7:14 which had a partial fulfillment in Isaiah's son, but that son (Isa. 8:1-3) was a type of the ultimate, antitypical Son (Isa. 9:6), the Messiah.[4]

The New Joshua

Perhaps the most explicit Old Testament indicator that Joshua is a type of the Messiah occurs in Isaiah 49:8. Isaiah records God's description of the work of the coming Messiah: "to cause them [God's people] to inherit the desolate heritages." Here the prophet uses the same Hebrew expression that we find repeatedly employed to portray the work of Joshua (see Deut. 31:7; Joshua 1:6). Thus the inspired writer indicates that Joshua, in his mission of causing ancient Israel to inherit the land of Canaan, is a type of the Messiah in His work of enabling spiritual Israel to inherit the antitypical land of Canaan.

What the Old Testament has already clearly announced—that Joshua is a type of Christ—we find verified in the New Testament proclamation, especially in Hebrews 4. Verses 8 and 9 pinpoint the typological connection: "For if Joshua [the KJV mistakenly has "Jesus" here, since in the Greek the two names are identical] had given them rest, then He [God] would not afterward have spoken of another day. There remains therefore a rest for the people of God." The comparison and contrast between Joshua and Jesus here indicate that Jesus is the antitypical Joshua, accomplishing in the antitype what the type only partially fulfilled.

Joshua in Type and Antitype

So far in our discussion of biblical typology in general, and the typology of Joshua in particular, we have focused on one important aspect: the inner biblical controls identifying and verifying that Joshua indeed was divinely ordained to be a type. Now we must move to another crucial control for the proper understanding of typology.

In my study of biblical typology for my doctoral dissertation, I was excited to learn that the Bible not only provides indicators that clearly *identify* the types but also gives controls for properly interpreting *how* each type will be fulfilled in the antitype.

The New Testament presents a consistent picture of how the Old Testament kingdom prophecies and types would meet their fulfillment in the "last days" (Heb. 1:1, 2) of the New Testament era. The New Testament perspective[5] visualizes one end-time fulfillment in three distinct phases, or aspects: (1) Christ's first advent, (2) the church, and (3) Christ's second advent and beyond.

The basic literal fulfillment centers in Jesus at His first advent: "All the promises of God [including the typological predictions] in Him are Yes, and in Him Amen" (2 Cor. 1:20). For example, Jesus is the antitypical Israel (Matt. 2:15), the antitypical Exodus (Matt. 1-5; Luke 9:31), and the antitypical temple (Matt. 12:6; John 1:14; 2:21).

The second aspect of antitypical fulfillment takes place in the church, both corporately and individually. As the spiritual body of Christ (1 Cor. 12:27; Eph. 1:22, 23; etc.), the church partakes spiritually of the fulfillment worked out by Christ. For example, the church is antitypical Israel (Gal. 6:16), experiences the antitypical Exodus (1 Cor. 10; Heb. 4; 2 Cor. 6:17), and becomes the temple of God (1 Cor. 3:16, 17; 2 Cor. 6:16).

Finally, the glorious consummated fulfillment of the types occurs in connection with the second advent of Christ and beyond, when the kingdom of grace becomes the kingdom of glory (Matt. 25:31) and the people of God are literally reunited with their King (1 Cor. 15:24; Heb. 9:28; 1 Peter 1:5; Rev. 21:3). To follow through on the examples already utilized above, apocalyptic Israel (Rev. 7:4; 14:1-5) will experience the ultimate exodus (Rev. 15:1-3) and dwell in the ultimate tabernacle/temple of God (Rev. 3:12; 7:15; 21:3, 22).

The chart on page 33 summarizes the three aspects of the New Testament fulfillment of typology, with examples:

What is true of all the other types of Scripture also applies to the typology of Joshua in his conquest of Canaan and dividing of the inheritance to Israel.

Joshua typology finds its basic literal fulfillment in connection with Jesus' first advent. As Joshua led Israel to Canaan after 40 years (Joshua 1-5), so the new Joshua entered heavenly Canaan after 40 days (Acts 1:3, 9-11; Heb. 1; 2). It was no coincidence that Jesus remained here on earth just 40 days after His resurrection. He was consciously following in the steps of Joshua—a day for a year—and at the end of the 40 days in the wilderness of this earth, He ascended to the heavenly Canaan as the "captain" or "pioneer" of our salvation (see Heb. 2:10). Just as Joshua conducted

Biblical Typology:
Three Aspects of New Testament Fulfillment

Old Testament Types	New Testament Antitypes		
Persons, Events, Institutions	Christ (Christological)	Church (Ecclesiological)	Final Climax (Apocalyptic)
Israel	New Israel (Matt. 2:15)	Israel of God (Gal. 6:16)	Apocalyptic Israel (Rev. 7:4)
Exodus	Christ's Exodus (Matt. 1-5; Luke 9:31)	Spiritual Exodus (Heb. 4; 2 Cor. 6:17)	Apocalyptic Exodus (Rev. 15:1-3)
Sanctuary/Temple	Christ as Temple (John 1:14; 2:21; Matt. 12:6)	Church as Temple (1 Cor. 3:16, 17; 2 Cor. 6:16)	Heavenly Temple/ Ultimate Temple (Rev. 3:12; 7:15; 11:19; 21:3, 22)

the conquest of Israel's enemies (Joshua 6-12), so Jesus led the conquest of our spiritual enemies (Col. 2:15). Just as the major goal of Joshua was to bring rest to the people of Israel (Joshua 1:13-15; 14:15; 21:44; 22:4; 23:1), so the antitypical Joshua says, "I will give you rest" (Matt. 11:28; see Heb. 4:8, 9). And just as Joshua appointed an inheritance for Israel (Joshua 1:6; 13-21), so the new Joshua, Jesus, receives and appoints an inheritance for His saints (Heb. 1:4; 9:15).

What is true of Jesus, the new Joshua, is also available to the church, members of His spiritual body. We also can come by faith to the heavenly Canaan (Heb. 12:22-24), conduct spiritual warfare against our spiritual enemies (Eph. 6:10-17), enjoy the spiritual rest of grace (Heb. 4:9-11; cf. *The SDA Bible Commentary*, Ellen G. White Comments, vol. 2, p. 928), and receive our spiritual inheritance (Acts 20:32; Eph. 1:11, 14, 18).

And the Joshua typology will one day reach its consummation in connection with the Second Advent and beyond. We will find literal entry into the Promised Land, heaven, and after 1,000 years the new earth (Rev. 20:9; 21:3). The final conquest of the enemies of God in the Promised Land will at last happen (Rev. 20:7-10; cf. Zech. 14; Eze. 38; 39), and we will enter final eternal rest in the earthly Canaan (Rev. 21; 22), where we can enjoy eternally our ultimate inheritance (Matt. 25:34; Col. 3:24; Rev. 21:7).

The following chart summarizes the threefold typology of Joshua:

The Threefold Typology of Joshua

Old Testament Joshua	Jesus	Church	End-Time
1. Leads Israel to Canaan after 40 years (Joshua 1-5)	Ascended to heavenly Canaan after 40 days (Acts 1:3, 9-11; Heb. 1; 2)	To Mount Zion by faith (Heb. 12: 22-24)	Literal entry into earthly Promised Land (Rev. 20:9; 21:2, 3)
2. Conducts conquest of Israel's enemies (Joshua 6-12)	Conducts conquest of Israel's enemies—principalities and powers (Col. 2:15)	Spiritual warfare (Eph. 6:10-27)	Final battle against the enemies of God (Rev. 20:7-10)
3. Leads Israel into God's rest (Joshua 1:13-15; 14:15; 21:44; 22:4; 23:1)	Brings rest (Matt. 11:28; Heb. 4)	Spiritual rest of grace (Heb. 4)	Final eternal rest in earthly Canaan (Rev. 21; 22)
4. Appoints the inheritance (Joshua 1:6; 13-21)	Receives and appoints an inheritance for His saints (Heb. 1:4; 9:15)	Receive spiritual inheritance (Acts 20:32; Eph. 1:11, 14, 18)	Final inheritance (Matt. 25:34; Col. 3:24; Rev. 21:7)

The book of Joshua contains a rich typology and a beautiful prophetic portrait of the work of our Saviour, Joshua-Jesus! What fantastic battle strategies and blessings it promises for us as spiritual Israel as we enter by faith into the heavenly Canaan and yet have many battles ahead to "possess our possessions"! What glorious portrayals of the final windup of the great controversy, the apportionment of our eternal inheritance, and our entry into ultimate rest!

Let us follow in Joshua's footsteps, for in so doing we are following the steps of our Saviour, Jesus!

[1] See my published dissertation, *Typology in Scripture: A Study of Hermeneutical Typos Structures,* Andrews University Seminary Doctoral Dissertation Series, vol. 2 (Berrien Springs, Mich.: Andrews University Press, 1981).

[2] See Saul Levin, *The Father of Joshua/Jesus* (Binghampton, N.Y.: State University of New York, 1978).

[3] See John Sailhamer, *The Pentateuch as Narrative* (Grand Rapids, Mich.: Zondervan, 1992), pp. 478, 479; idem., class notes for the doctoral seminar in "Old Testament Interpretation: Intertextuality," Trinity Evangelical Divinity School, Fall 1993.

[4] See Richard Davidson, "New Testament Use of the Old Testament," *Journal of the Adventist Theological Society* 5, No. 1 (1994): 17-19.

[5] See Davidson, *Typology in Scripture,* pp. 390-397; "Sanctuary Typology," *Symposium on Revelation—Book I,* Daniel and Revelation Committee Series, ed. Frank B. Holbrook (Silver Spring, Md.: Biblical Research Institute, 1992), vol. 6, pp. 106-111, 129.

Battle Strategy

3

The book of Joshua gives the definitive Old Testament typologi-cal model for "victorious living." The preparation, the battle strategies for conquering spiritual enemies, the source of strength and success, the causes of setbacks, and the divine remedy—this book has them all. In this chapter we focus upon the keynote of the book that encapsulates the whole message of Joshua, which follows. Here God Himself gives to Joshua, and to us, the divine battle strategy for victory and success in our spiritual warfare.

"Wednesday, April 13, noon. I stand upon Mount Nebo looking down below me to the Jordan Valley. I imagine Joshua camped at the acacia grove, just northeast of the Dead Sea, after the death of Moses. In my mind's eye I see him almost over-whelmed by his new responsibilities as leader of Israel and awed by the tasks that lay ahead. How was he to cross the swollen Jordan, to conquer the walled cities, to slay the giants? How could he successfully subdue the land? Then I consider God's solution to Joshua's problem. . . ."

In chapter 1 God outlines *four clear*, *practical*, *powerful* components in the divine battle strategy.

Undaunted Courage

The first is so important that God repeats it three times in ever-increasing intensity:

"Be strong and of good courage" (verse 6).

36

"Only be strong and very courageous" (verse 7).
"Have I not commanded you? Be strong and of good courage; do not be afraid, nor be dismayed" (verse 9).

Already when Moses had handed over the reins of leadership, he had given to Joshua the same message twice before: "Be strong and of good courage" (Deut. 31:7, 23). That's five times. And at the end of Joshua 1, the people add a sixth time as they say to their new leader: "Only be strong and of good courage." And for the seventh and last time in the Joshua narratives, during the southern campaign, Joshua says to the captains of his army, "Be strong and of good courage" (Joshua 10:25).

In response to Joshua's temptation to be discouraged, frightened, and dismayed, God commands—*"Be strong and of good courage!"* Or as the rich Hebrew terms can be literally translated: Be *firm/courageous/confident* and *be bold!* The first divine prerequisite for success and victory is undaunted *courage, confidence,* and *boldness.*

While in my first district as a young pastor, I had the privilege of working with Ron Halvorsen, a former gang leader in New York City, who understood this principle. He was then Faith for Today evangelist, and my conference president had secured his services for a whole monthlong crusade in our little mountain town of Flagstaff, Arizona. I was scared to death at the prospect of his coming. A rather timid young pastor, I found it difficult to go out to meet new people. I didn't have that many evangelistic interests and had already held one campaign on my own—and it was not what you would call a booming numerical success.

When Ron Halvorsen came storming into town, he sensed my timidity and tendency to be disheartened, and promptly gave me a nickname. He never again called me Dick, but rather "holy boldness"! Repeatedly he would say, "Come on, 'holy boldness,' let's go!"

Just a few years ago, shortly after I had begun teaching at the Seventh-day Adventist Theological Seminary, Elder Halvorsen gave a Week of Prayer in our seminary chapel. Standing up to speak the first day, he looked up in the balcony where I sat and blurted out, "Well, if it isn't 'holy boldness!'" He had not forgotten, nor have I. I haven't forgotten the power generated by Halvorsen's undaunted courage and boldness for the Lord. To my amazement, our little church with a regular attendance of 40 or so members had 40 more join our ranks through baptism.

But Ron Halvorsen's courage did not come by trusting his own capabilities. He was continually telling stories on himself of his own stumbling, bungling ways. And my courage did not come by simply the reception of a nickname. Elder Halvorsen could call me "holy boldness" till he was blue in the face, and that wouldn't make me courageous. The power of positive thinking does not by itself produce holy boldness. God could command Joshua, "Be strong and very courageous." But the wherewithal was not in Joshua's own abilities.

If we look closely at the biblical text, however, we discover a second principle, the *secret* of courage, of holy boldness for the Lord. But it is not courage or confidence in ourselves.

Unwavering Confidence in Divine Promises

Every time God commands Joshua to be courageous, He couples the command with a *divine promise*. So in verses 3-5, before the command for courage, God promises: "Every place that the sole of your foot will tread upon I have given you, as I said to Moses. . . . No man shall be able to stand before you all the days of your life; as I was with Moses, so I will be with you. I will not leave you nor forsake you" (verses 3-5).

Again in verse 9 the wherewithal promise follows the command to be courageous: "For the Lord your God is with you wherever you go." Joshua's undaunted courage came, not from his own resources, but from claiming God's unfailing promises.

It was in college that I first learned about claiming Bible promises. In a seminar we learned about the ABCs of the prayer of reception based upon the biblical steps of ask, believe, and claim: *asking* God to fulfill His promise (see Matt. 21:22); telling Him "*I believe* Your promise" (see Mark 11:24); and *claiming* the promise, thanking God that He has already answered my prayer (see John 11:41).

Soon I began to experience the power of God's promises. I remember coming into a Bible class for a major exam. Although I had studied hard, now I just blanked out. I looked at the test and couldn't remember the answer to a single question. Then I took a deep breath and claimed God's promise in John 14:26 about bringing to my memory the things Christ has taught me. As I thanked God for already answering my prayer, I looked back at the test. The questions at the bottom of the page were still a blank, but as I started at the top and came to each question in turn, it was as if Someone lifted a veil and the answer became clear. For each question the miracle reoccurred, the power of the promise unleashed.

I wish I had the rest of this book to bear testimony to the power of God's promises. I remember bouts with insomnia in college. Stressed out, I found myself unable to sleep for hours at a time. One night after tossing and turning, I remembered God's promise in Proverbs 3:24: "Yes, you will lie down and your sleep will be sweet." And in Psalm 127:2: "For so He gives His beloved sleep." Kneeling beside the bed, I claimed these promises, and when I got back in bed, what happened was how I imagine it would feel if a dozen tranquilizers all took effect at one time. Layers of stress peeled away instantly. Within seconds I was asleep. The results of claiming God's promises have sometimes been dramatic, sometimes not. I realize my insomnia was only a symptom from unresolved stress, and God is gradually teaching me (as I allow Him) to handle the stress by turning it over to Him. But I've persevered through colporteuring, through seminary training, through my years of pastoring, and now teaching with my "power pack" of promises from the Bible and the writings of Ellen White.

When I faced my professors for my doctoral dissertation defense, I claimed again and again the promise of Isaiah 50:7: "The Lord God will help me; therefore shall I not be confounded: therefore have I set my face like a flint, and I know that I shall not be ashamed" (KJV). I found God giving me a calm and poise and presence of mind far beyond my own powers.

Recently I faced depression and discouragement for a number of reasons, and I had an anxiety attack as I lay in bed with the flu. I couldn't pull myself out of depression and anxiety on my own. But I went to my power pack—of index cards with favorite promises from the Bible and the writings of Ellen White. Saturating my mind with the promises brought back courage!

I've found an encouraging Bible or Ellen White promise for every situation—promises for studying, decision-making, worry, tiredness, lack of concentration, bad memory, despondency, bad temper, sickness, failure, etc. According to one count, the Bible has more than 3,500 promises suited to all our needs. Add to this the insight that "all His biddings are enablings" *(Christ's Object Lessons,* p. 333), and the number of biblical promises is almost unlimited!

Joshua had his power pack. Armed with the divine promises in the Word of God, the book of the Law, the *courage* of Joshua, and Israel was undaunted. The river Jordan parted before them. The walls of Jericho collapsed before their courageous shout. Their enemies melted in fear and were utterly defeated as the Lord fought for Israel as He had promised. At the end of Joshua's victorious campaigns, he could testify as to God's unfailing promises (Joshua 21:43-45).

I haven't been as constant in claiming God's promises as I should have. I'm ashamed at all the blessings I've forfeited. Yet I have experienced enough that I can second Joshua's testimony to the *power of undaunted courage* based upon *claiming the unfailing promises* of God.

In recent years I've gotten into the habit of asking those I meet, "How's your courage?" Usually I give a parting farewell to those who visit me in my office: *"Courage!"* Perhaps the habit has come from my own struggle against discouragement. But recently I discovered similar counsel in Ellen White's writings: "Send along the line God's message to His workers: 'Be strong and of a good courage'" *(Testimonies,* vol. 7, p. 185).

By experience I have confirmed her further counsel: "A discouraged soul is filled with darkness, shutting out the light of God from his own soul and casting a shadow upon the pathway of others" *(Steps to Christ,* p. 117). And I am comforted by her own call to courage based in the divine promises: "Again I say: Be of good courage. Trust in the Lord. Let not the enemy rob you of the promises" *(Testimonies,* vol. 2, p. 593).

Undaunted courage and unwavering confidence in the promises of God—they are the first two steps in God's divine battle strategy. The third principle follows on their heels.

Unreserved Commitment to God's Will

"That you may observe to do according to all the law which Moses My servant commanded you; do not turn from it to the right hand or to the left, that you may prosper wherever you go" (Joshua 1:7). God calls Joshua also to *unreserved commitment* to His will as the basis for true success and victory in his spiritual warfare.

The book of Joshua testifies how God can bless those who have total consecration to the will of God. As Israel moved forward in the path of obedience, enemies were conquered and giants slain. At the same time the stories of Achan and Ai and the Valley of Achor witness eloquently to the failure that results from compromise with sin.

Likewise, we see the results of Israel's later failure to follow through on Joshua's conquest. Joshua had *taken* the whole land, but much remained to be fully possessed. According to the record in Joshua 17:13—"When the people of Israel grew strong, . . . they put the Canaanites to forced labor, but did not utterly drive them out." The book of Judges and the rest of the Old Testament show the result in apostasy from that failure to wholly follow God's command. Already at the end of Joshua's life he saw the trend in Israel's experience, and in the covenant renewal ceremony he charged his people to take a decided stand: "Choose for yourselves this day whom you will serve, whether the gods which your fathers served that were on the other side of the River, or the gods of the Amorites, in whose land you dwell. But as for me and my house, we will serve the Lord" (Joshua 24:15).

The same call goes out to my heart and to all God's family today. The new Joshua says, choose—whether the gold and Babylonish garments, riches and fashion, of Achan, or the eternal treasure. The gods of this world or the God of the universe. The giants and Canaanites: Will we let them remain in our lives, or will we utterly exterminate or drive them out?

We face moral giants—impurity, lust, passion. Will it be compromise and coexistence and corruption, or entire surrender? We have the promise: "The surrender of all our powers to God greatly simplifies the problem of life. It weakens and cuts short a thousand struggles with the passions of the natural heart" *(Messages to Young People*, p. 30).

Intellectual giants threaten us. An Adventist writer not too long ago compared the higher critical approach toward Scripture with that of Adventist scholars in the land of the giants. Amazingly, the author explicitly continued the analogy, but suggested we should "tame" the critical giants. Does Scripture call for just *taming* the giants? Is the giant of setting our reason as supreme over Scripture just to be put on a leash, or to be exterminated in our personal experience? Read Joshua 11:20 carefully!

Still other giants in our lives challenge us—difficulties, problems, temptations. Will we as an Adventist family choose *this day* to wholly follow the Lord as did Joshua and his house?

I find I need every morning to make a trek to my quiet place and kneel before God with this prayer: "Take me, O Lord, as wholly Thine. I lay all my plans at Thy feet. Use me today in Thy service. Abide with me, and let all my work be wrought in Thee" *(Steps to Christ*, p. 70). Without that daily surrender and consecration to unswerving obedience, I have no power against the giants in my life.

And this leads us to the final step in God's battle strategy for success and victory. We cannot maintain *unreserved commitment* to God's will on our own. Neither could Joshua. And so God gives the fourth part of the battle strategy.

Uninterrupted Communion

"This Book of the Law shall not depart from your mouth, but you shall meditate in it day and night, that you may observe to do according to all that is written in it. For then you will make your way prosperous, and then you will have good success" (Joshua 1:8).

If we wish to maintain unreserved commitment to God's will, we must have *uninterrupted communion* with Him. "This Book of the Law shall not depart out of your mouth, but you shall *meditate* in it day and night, *[in order]* that [the result may come] you may observe to do according to all that is written in it." The source of Joshua's power for obedience was his life of prayer and meditation. As Ellen G. White put it: "What was Joshua's victory? Thou shalt meditate upon the Word of God day and night. The word of the Lord came to Joshua just before he passed over Jordan. . . . [Joshua 1:7, 8 quoted.] This was the secret of Joshua's victory. He made God his Guide" *(The SDA Bible Commentary,* Ellen G. White Comments, vol. 2, p. 993). Compare this with one of my favorite promises found in my power pack:

"Walk continually in the light of God. Meditate day and night upon His character. Then you will see His beauty and rejoice in His goodness. Your heart will glow with a sense of His love. You will be uplifted as if borne by everlasting arms. With the power and light that God imparts, you can comprehend more and accomplish more than you ever before deemed possible" *(The Ministry of Healing,* p. 514).

"Comprehend more and accomplish more than you ever before deemed possible"—that's relevant for all of us whatever our walk of life! I can bear testimony that this battle strategy works. But here is where I still so often fall short. I fear that many of us are too often so busy doing many good things—studying, working, taking care of our families—that the most important thing of all, quality and quantity time with God, gets shortchanged. Satan is happy to get us sidetracked into anything—as long as it eliminates time for meditation.

I have found that my efficiency and victory are directly proportional to the time I spend on intense meditation and communion with God. When I become irritable, short-tempered, or depressed, or when I begin to fall into any of the numerous other temptation traps the enemy has prepared for me, it inevitably comes down to my trying to get by without time for devotions.

The book of Joshua gives us a rich picture of the life of meditation. In its etymology the Hebrew word for "meditate" used in Joshua 1:8 literally means "to give forth sighs." We get a word picture of pouring over God's Word until the sighs of contentment begin to spontaneously come forth: "Ah!" *"Wow!"*

And it is to be a continual experience. "Meditate day and night" implies the memorizing of Scripture so that we can constantly ruminate upon it like a cow chews its cud—digesting, then bringing up to chew on again. The clause "this Book of the Law shall not depart out of your mouth" recalls this word picture of ruminating, which literally means "chewing the cud."

The subject matter of meditation is significant. It is not the

Eastern variety of looking within oneself, but rather of focusing on Scripture. In Joshua's time the only Scripture was *Torah,* often translated Law, but including the whole Pentateuch. The Torah that Joshua was to meditate on contained commands and promises. We have seen how we can claim the promises. Every command also became an enabling that Joshua carried out.

The Torah also contained some 50 chapters describing the sanctuary and its services—foreshadowings of the gospel realities. Already we have noted how in the center of each of the two halves of the book of Joshua—the two high points—we find Joshua setting up the altar and the tabernacle. The gospel is the central focus in the book of Joshua and should be also in our meditation.

The Torah also contained narratives of how God had delivered His people in the past, and Joshua learned how to make such sections relevant by the principle of *personalization.* As we will study in detail in our final chapter, on Joshua 24, God recounts the story of the Exodus with the alternating phrases: *Your fathers* came out of Egypt, and *you* came to the sea, and *your fathers* were pursued by the Egyptians, but the Lord put darkness between *you* and them. You—your fathers. Who really came out of Egypt? Very few of the generation that heard these words had actually left Egypt, but God showed that the later generation was to *personalize* the story, to consider as if it had happened to them.

We have briefly noted some of the crucial elements of meditation that emerge from Joshua—memorization, rumination, and personalization. Just now, fellow pilgrim in the footsteps of Joshua, shall we make a new commitment to priority *meditation*—intense personal communion with God? Shall we determine not to enter each day's activities unless we have gone with Joshua to our spiritual Gilgal to commune personally with God? As students of the Word—shall we make first priority the source of our power?

Good Success

I can testify that God's battle strategy has really worked in my life when I have dared to put it into practice. I commend to you the way of (1) *undaunted courage* based upon (2) *unwavering confidence* in claiming the promises of God; (3) *unreserved commit-*

ment to God's will flowing from (4) *uninterrupted communion* in His presence. If you like mnemonic devices, take hold of the four-fold "UC"—the letters that start each of the four steps—and indeed it will be true that you ["u"] will see ["c"] the fulfillment of God's promise to those who follow His strategy: "*Then* you will make your way prosperous, and then you will have *good success.*" He means what He says. Shall we take Him at His word?

Reconnaissance

--------------------------------- **4** ---------------------------------

Monday, April 25, 4:30 p.m. We are now approaching Jericho, the City of the Palms, the lowest city in the world (820 feet below sea level), and according to archaeologists, also the oldest. Even though it is still springtime, it is already very hot. The fertile plain surrounding Jericho has a subtropical climate, producing dates, bananas, and other tropical fruits. The modern city of Jericho appears as an oasis of green, with the groves of palm trees and banana plants, well watered (at least in part) by the copious spring—'Elisha's spring' (see 2 Kings 2:18-22)—that still bubbles up near the ancient city of Old Testament times.

"Tell es-Sulțân, or Old Testament Jericho, at the northwestern edge of the modern city of Jericho, an artificial mound (or tell) some 10 acres in size, was not a large city by modern standards, or by standards of Mesopotamian or Egyptian cities. Nonetheless, it was large (see *Patriarchs and Prophets*, p. 487) compared with other Canaanite walled cities of the time, and it was certainly strategically located. It stood just opposite the main fords of the Jordan River and guarded the access routes up through the wilderness into the central highlands of Palestine and beyond. Thus Jericho 'was virtually the key to the whole country' *(ibid.*, p. 482).

"I imagine the two spies slipping quietly into the city just before the gates close. I also enter the gate to the tell before closing time. I walk along the crest around the tell, where the ancient walls were. Erosion in this subtropical climate of the Jordan Valley has not left many remains intact, but I recall the recent reinterpretation of excavation data that illuminates the biblical account.[1] I examine the squares and trenches that archaeologists have cut down from the crest at the edge of the tell to the lowest spots at its base. These excavations have exposed evidence for a double wall of the Late Bronze Age city of Rahab's time, which included a lower revetment wall at the base of the tell, built of stone some 15 feet high and topped with a mud-brick parapet wall and an upper mud-brick wall at the crest of the ramparts. The remains of lower-class houses (with walls only one brick thick) were found built between the upper and lower walls. Though little or no remains are now visible because of the erosion since the first excavations, I think especially of the houses built inside against the lower wall, with their foundations abutting the stone revetment wall and with windows cut into the mud-brick parapet, and remember how Rahab lived 'in the city wall' (Joshua 2:15, literal translation).

"I go to the edge of the tell, perhaps to the spot where Rahab's house was. From this location, I look over to Jebel Qaranṭal (the traditional location of Jesus' wilderness temptations) and other precipitous cliffs about a mile west of Jericho, full of crevasses and caves, in one of which the spies probably hid for several days. I reflect on the story of the spies and Rahab. . . ."

From the account of the two spies, we can learn important typological lessons. For the new Christian contemplating entrance into spiritual Canaan, into the "rest of grace," this narrative teaches the necessity of "counting the cost" of what it means to inherit the full blessing in Christ. We learn the importance of conducting reconnaissance missions before launching our attack against the enemy. Christians need to be wise to the wiles of Satan in order to successfully encounter and defeat him through God's power.

A Classic Spy Story

While I do not want to diminish the value of the foregoing truths, I'd like to suggest that the heart of the narrative of Joshua 2 lies elsewhere. Let's look more closely.

Joshua 2 is a classic spy story. Not just true-to-life fiction, as many spy stories go (and as many critical scholars claim for this account), but a spy story that really happened as recorded.[2]

The Bible contains several such stories (Num. 13; Joshua 2; Judges 18). The account in Joshua 2 has many allusions to the narrative of the 12 spies in Numbers 13. Both stories begin with the same command, "Go, view [spy] the land" (Joshua 2:1; cf. Num. 13:2). Joshua sends out two spies, echoing the two faithful spies of Numbers 13. Clearly, the biblical writer presents Joshua 2 as a spy story, like Numbers 13.

What are the essential elements of a spy story, according to Numbers 13?[3]

1. The spies are commissioned (Num. 13:1-20).
2. The spies enter the land (verses 21, 22).
3. The spies locate an item of value (verses 23, 24).
4. The spies return to the people (verse 25).
5. The spies present the item of value (verse 26).
6. The spies report on their findings (verses 27-29).
7. Someone makes a decision to act on the basis of the report (verses 30-33).

Many of these elements are immediately apparent in the spy story of Joshua 2. Note the parallels:

1. Joshua commissions and sends the spies (Joshua 2:1).
2. The spies enter the land selected for reconnaissance (verse 1).
4. The spies return to the people (verses 22, 23).
6. They report on their findings (verses 23, 24).
7. Leadership makes a decision to act on the basis of the report (Joshua 3-6).

What is particularly intriguing, however, is that two crucial aspects of the Numbers 13 spy story at first glance appear missing in Joshua 2—numbers 3 and 5 in the list. The spies at Jericho find no item of value in their reconnaissance mission, nothing to present upon their return to the people.

Or do they? Upon closer inspection of the story, we see that two elements are not missing after all. The two spies do find an item of value. That item is Rahab herself! It is true that the spies do not bring her back immediately, but before the story is over, in Joshua 6, Rahab is brought to the people, eventually into the midst of Israel, valued and embraced by the covenant community, and ultimately becoming one of the progenitors of the Messiah!

The "Item of Value": Rahab!

The heart of the Jericho spy story is the finding of the item of value—Rahab. I see seven beautiful facets of the valuable jewel Rahab scintillating from the narrative:

1. Rahab is valued as a "diamond in the rough." Far from perfect, she was a prostitute and not hesitant to tell a lie when she thought it necessary. But God received her as she was, accepted her faith on the level of her knowledge and experience. Like a diamond in the rough, she appeared a most unlikely candidate to be God's "item of value" in the spy story. But her life gives encouragement to all of us. God wants to save and use mightily even the apparently least-promising individuals.

2. Rahab is valued as a treasured testimony to the mercy of God upon all humanity, even upon the so-called heathen. In Genesis 15 God told Abram that the inhabitants of Canaan would have 400 years of probation because "the iniquity of the Amorites is not yet complete" (verse 16). During the intervening centuries we have some evidence that God's Spirit was active among them, that He had left a witness for them to follow (for example, Melchizedek and Balaam). Rahab's experience shows clearly that inhabitants of Canaan living just before the conquest had opportunity to learn the truth about Yahweh: "He is God in heaven above and on earth beneath" (Joshua 2:11).

In fact, Rahab's testimony of faith to the spies reveals an amazingly mature understanding of the character of Israel's God. As Jon Berquist puts it: "Rahab makes one of the most impassioned and logical statements of any kind throughout the book of Joshua (verses 9-13). The spies fade into the woodwork of the brothel wall while Rahab lectures them about the faith in God that enables victories."[4] Do our lives give such a brilliant testimony to God's character?

3. Rahab is valued for her awesome courage. She is willing to stand alone against the whole culture that surrounds her. In the midst of the prevailing Canaanite religion, she accepts a new God, a Deity totally opposed to the moon god of her city and all the other fertility gods of her land.

The woman knew that if the king of Jericho found out that she had helped the spies he would regard her as a traitor, and she with her family would face immediate execution. Yet she was willing to take the terrible risk to rescue the spies. In contrast with the other inhabitants of Jericho, whose "hearts melted" and "neither did there remain any more courage in anyone" (verse 11), Rahab courageously follows the God of Israel.

Are we willing to stand alone against the prevailing secular, anti-Christian culture of modern Western society? Are we willing to risk our own lives and the lives of our family for the sake of God in order to help those in desperate need? Oh, that the Christian church today had the courage of Rahab!

4. Rahab is valued for her faith. The heart of the Rahab narrative within the Jericho spy story is this—Rahab believed! The author of the Epistle to the Hebrews highlights her faith in his hall of biblical fame: "By faith the harlot Rahab did not perish with those who did not believe, when she had received the spies with peace" (Heb. 11:31). It is remarkable that the apostle James chooses only two Old Testament figures to illustrate the nature of active faith—Abraham, the "friend of God" (James 2:21-24), and "Rahab the harlot" (verse 25).

As the apostle James recognizes, Rahab's experience is one of the most singular, balanced examples of righteousness by faith in all of Scripture. Basing her response upon the report of God's mighty acts in behalf of Israel—their deliverance from Egypt, crossing the Red Sea, and conquering the Amorite kings east of the Jordan—Rahab trusts in Yahweh as "God in heaven above and on earth beneath" (Joshua 2:11), even when she had not personally witnessed any evidence of Yahweh's activity. Yet her trust does not reflect a mere passive acceptance of an abstract truth. It led to action—works made her faith active as she received and hid the spies, and sent them out to safety.

While we note the faith of Rahab in this story, at the same time we must not overlook the faith of the two spies! Though not mentioned in faith's hall of fame in Hebrews 11, yet their faith is also remarkable. When vowing to Rahab to show her *hesed* (covenant loyalty or faithful kindness), they do not say, "*If* the Lord gives us the land . . . ," but "*When* the Lord has given us the land . . ." (verse 14). In contrast to the cowardly report of the 10 spies some 40 years earlier, these two faithful spies tell Joshua, "Truly the Lord has delivered all the land into our hands" (verse 24)!

Is our faith "made perfect" by works of care and helping concern for those in need? Are we able to say of the upcoming spiritual battles in our lives "Truly the Lord has delivered all the land into our hands"?

5. Rahab is valued as an agent of salvation. She saves the Israelite spies, hiding them at great personal risk to herself and her family. Her speech to the spies is actually an oracle of salvation for all Israel. She announces, "I know that the Lord has given you the land" (verse 9). Rahab also becomes an agent of salvation for her whole family as she asks the Israelites to show steadfast love or lovingkindness (Hebrew *hesed*) to all her next of kin.

The narrative especially highlights the redemptive nature of Rahab's actions in the spies' many allusions to the Passover as they stipulate what Rahab should do. Donald Madvig points out the "striking similarities to the Passover: compare the scarlet cord with the sprinkled blood and the requirement that Rahab's family remain in the house with the command that the Passover be eaten in family units and that no one was to leave the house (Ex. 12:21-23)."[5]

Beyond these thematic parallels we also find terminological similarities. Both instances refer to a "sign" (Hebrew, *'ôt)* (Ex. 12:13; Joshua 2:12)—the "true token" Rahab requests of the spies. Note also the virtually exact language in the prohibition not to leave the house: "None of you shall go out of the door of his house" (Ex. 12:22); "Whoever goes outside the doors of your house . . ." (Joshua 2:19). Finally, both incidents employ the term *blood:* the blood of the substitute lamb at the Passover (Ex. 12:13) and the blood upon the heads of those who did not remain in Rahab's house under the sign of the scarlet cord (Joshua 2:19). All of these parallels connect the scarlet cord with the blood of the Passover lamb, and provide biblical basis for a typological interpretation.

It is especially intriguing to observe that the Hebrew word for "cord" used in the Joshua narrative is *tiqwāh*, which everywhere else in the Hebrew Bible—31 times—means "hope." The biblical author seems to be employing a play on words in this story: the scarlet cord hung by Rahab signifies the source of redemptive hope for the spies, for Israel, for Rahab and her household, and ultimately—as the cord, like the blood of the Paschal lamb, typologically prefigures Christ—for the whole world! Are you under the sign of the scarlet cord, the sign of hope through the blood of Jesus?

6. Rahab is valued as an integral part of Israel's community. When the Israelite soldiers rescue her after the collapse of Jericho's walls, they temporarily bring her to the outside edge of the Israelite camp, perhaps for a time of instruction and purification. But soon this period comes to an end.

As the final climax to the spies-and-Rahab narrative, "Joshua spared Rahab the harlot, her father's household, and all that she had. So she dwells in Israel to this day" (Joshua 6:25). The Hebrew literally reads that she dwells "in the midst [b*qere_b_]" of Israel. Berquist comments insightfully on this Hebrew phrase b*qere_b_, "in the midst": "The term refers to inward parts, or even the womb. Rahab the prostitute now enters the womb of Israel and the story reaches its second climax. The community enfolds Rahab."[6]

The name Rahab in Hebrew is also an adjective meaning "wide" or "broad," and is related to the adjective r*ḥôb, "[city] square or open place." As the city square was often either at the gate of the city or in the heart of the city, where the elders conducted the business affairs of the city, so Rahab, who had been marginalized on the lower walls of Jericho, is now welcomed into the heart and hub of the life of Israel.

The 12 spies some 38 years earlier had brought back the cluster of grapes, so the two spies now also eventually returned with "fruit" from their reconnaissance mission: Rahab and her father's household now were the item of value, the ultimate fruit! Do we value and enfold the "Rahabs" who join our church?

7. Rahab is valued as an ancestor of Christ. A comparison of several biblical passages (see Num. 7:12; Ruth 4:18-22; 1 Chron. 2:11, 12; Matt. 1:1, 5-6) reveals that Rahab married Salmon, son of Nahshon, one of the prominent princes of Judah, and she gave birth to Boaz, great-grandfather of David. Thus Rahab the harlot becomes an ancestor of the Messiah!

Is it appropriate that God would allow Rahab to be part of the Messianic lineage? Yes, indeed! Note that Matthew's genealogy of Christ mentions five women, and moral charges were leveled against all of them. God takes Tamar, woman of prostitution and incest,

Rahab the harlot, Ruth the Moabitess, Bathsheba the adulteress, and Mary the virgin with child. Each of these women, justly or falsely accused of moral impropriety (in Ruth's case because of her national identity), believed in the coming Messiah and were sinners cleansed by the blood of the One who would come through their lineage.

We too, once spiritual harlots because of our unfaithfulness to God, may be part of the seed of Abraham and part of the spiritual seed of the Messianic line. All of us, like Rahab, have been spiritually promiscuous and deserving of death. But if we choose to believe in the God of heaven above and the earth beneath, if we choose to come under the sign of the scarlet cord, to remain under the blood of the Lamb, we find ourselves welcomed into the family of God, into the midst of His covenant people—and not only become spiritual members of the Messianic lineage, but part of the very body of Christ!

"I stand on Tell es-Sulṭân, ancient Jericho, and look down at the eroded remains of where Rahab's house may have stood in the ancient revetment wall. Then I gaze eastward a few miles down to the location of ancient Gilgal, on the western bank of the Jordan River, where Rahab was welcomed into the camp of Israel after the fall of Jericho. She made the right choice—to side with God's people, no matter the cost! I reaffirm my commitment to side with the God of heaven and earth."

Would you, just now, like to do the same?

---

[1] See especially Bryant G. Wood, "Did the Israelites Conquer Jericho? A New Look at the Archaeological Evidence," *Biblical Archaeological Review,* March/April 1990, pp. 45-57.

[2] Critical scholars often use the term *story* to refer to a fictional account, but I use this word to mean a true, historical account that happened just as narrated by the inspired biblical writer.

[3] For this analysis, I am particularly indebted to Jon L. Berquist, "Expectations and Repeated Climax in the Rahab Story," paper presented at the AAR/SBL annual meeting, San Francisco, Nov. 23, 1992, although I do not subscribe to many of the critical conclusions reached by the presenter.

[4] *Ibid.,* p. 3.

[5] Donald H. Madvig, "Joshua," *The Expositor's Bible Commentary,* ed. Frank E. Gaebelein (Grand Rapids: Zondervan, 1992), vol. 3, p. 263.

[6] Berquist, pp. 4, 5.

Crossing
to Conquer

5

Wednesday, April 13, early morning. As I write these lines, we are just crossing the Jordan River at the Allenby Bridge, very near if not at the location where Joshua and the children of Israel crossed. The 'mighty Jordan' is now hardly bigger than a canal, since most of the flow from the Sea of Galilee goes to supply drinking and agricultural water instead of being wasted by flowing down the Jordan into the Dead Sea.

"It is no more the 'jungle of the Jordan' as in biblical times, although there are considerable scrub bushes and trees along the Jordan banks as we cross. . . .

"Springtime at the Jordan River. In ancient times spring brought the melting of the snows on Mount Hermon and the Lebanon Mountains, which swelled the tributaries of the Jordan above the Sea of Galilee. The excess water in the Sea of Galilee surged down the Jordan valley, overflowing the banks of the Jordan River, making passage at the usual fords impossible for large numbers of people.

"It is also springtime as we cross the Jordan River. Although we don't face the obstacle of impassable waters, the difficulties are still present, and the miracles just as great. . . .

"We have already been occupied more than two hours going through the Israeli border exit procedure (between Israel and Jordan),[1] and we still await the check by the Jordanian officials. Some of our multinational group of students (representing 10 different countries) wait their turn with trepidation because their passports have an Israeli stamp. Normally this would eliminate any possibility of entering into Jordan even though they have a valid Jordanian visa. They had no choice but to get the Israeli stamp since they had to be issued their visas before arrival in Israel.

"As we are waiting, I think of the formidable obstacles that confronted the armies of Israel at this river and the mighty miracle God performed in making possible a passage. I pray fervently and witness a miracle of passage not unlike the time of Joshua! As the Jordanian officials proceed with their check of passports, our Russian brother Rostislav, professor at the Seventh-day Adventist Zaokski Theological Seminary, hands his passport to the inspector who thumbs through it quickly, his attention diverted by one of the children in an adjoining seat, and never sees the page with the Israeli stamp. Our Turkish sister Melek has the same experience with a second official. He looks at every page of all passports around her, but coming to her passport, he hastily glances at a few pages and misses the page with the Israeli stamp.

"But the waters of the Jordan have not yet parted, however, for at the final border crossing check they take our passports and check them once more. My heart pounds as someone spots Rostislav's Israeli stamp. The official remarks grimly, 'Big problem.' Rostislav pleads to the official to be allowed to enter Jordan. I again pray that God will perform a modern-day miracle of crossing at the Jordan. The official disappears for a long time, and we are all praying for supernatural intervention as in Joshua's day. The man finally returns and speaks to Rostislav. We find that he has placed a special telephone call to the Jordanian minister of the interior himself, to intercede in Rostislav's behalf, and the minister has granted special permission for him to pass. Praise be to God—the Jordan River still parts for His people. A way of miraculous crossing is still occurring!"

Typology of the Crossings

Perhaps the most climactic event of the whole book of Joshua comes not at the end, but near the beginning. The crossing of the Jordan River culminates the great redemptive work of God that began at the Exodus. Israel came out of Egypt so that they could enter and possess the Promised Land (see Deut. 6:23). Miracles of passage occur both at the beginning and end of the journey to Canaan. Just as the people of Israel finally "believed the Lord and His servant Moses" after the crossing of the Red Sea (Ex. 14:31), so God promised to Joshua on the day of the Jordan passage: "This day I will begin to magnify you in the sight of all Israel, that they may know that, as I was with Moses, so I will be with you" (Joshua 3:7).

The parallels between the crossing of the Red Sea at the start of the Exodus and crossing the Jordan River at its close are hardly accidental. The psalmist, in his inspired intertextual interpretation of past events of divine deliverance, couples the two miracles in the same verse, as if part of a single event in salvation history: "The sea saw it and fled; Jordan turned back" (Ps. 114:3). Two verses later we find the same joining of crossings into one motif of deliverance: "What ails you, O sea, that you fled? O Jordan, that you turned back?" (verse 5).

The crossings of both the Red Sea and the Jordan thus form part of a single typological motif. Passing through the waters of the Jordan, like passing through the Red Sea, is a type of Christian baptism. Jesus Himself combines the two aspects of this typology as He undergoes His antitypical "Red Sea" experience by His baptism in the Jordan River.[2]

Paul wrote that all of ancient Israel "were baptized into Moses in the cloud and in the Sea" (1 Cor. 10:2). In a similar way, as it is part of the same typology, Israel was baptized into Joshua in the Jordan River. Hebrews 3 and 4 show that the entrance into literal Canaan typified the entry into the "rest of grace" through Jesus, the new Joshua. The narrative of Israel's crossing into Canaan thus offers a rich source of spiritual insight, as it typologically reveals the beginning of the Christian "rest of grace." We cross into spiritual Canaan through baptism and experiential understanding of righteousness by faith.[3]

At the same time, the Jordan crossing into Canaan finds its ultimate antitypical fulfillment in our final entry into heavenly Canaan. The ways ancient Israel prepared for crossing into Canaan thus also instruct God's people on the borders of heavenly Canaan, in the final days of earth's history before Jesus comes.

CROSSING TO CONQUER

Preparations for Passage

Like a refrain throughout the book of Joshua come the words: "Joshua rose early in the morning" (Joshua 3:1; 6:12; 7:16; 8:10). At the beginning of Joshua's career as leader of Israel, God instructed him, "You shall meditate in it [the Torah] day and night" (Joshua 1:8). It is evident that he cultivated the habit of rising early to commune with God in meditation and prayer. Ellen White states the source of Joshua's power (in the context of a later battle in which the sun stood still): "The man who commanded, 'Sun, stand thou still upon Gibeon; and thou, Moon, in the valley of Ajalon,' is the man who for hours lay prostrate upon the earth in prayer in the camp at Gilgal. The men of prayer are the men of power" *(Patriarchs and Prophets*, p. 509). (We will see a beautiful example of Joshua's devotional life at Gilgal in our next chapter.)

Those contemplating the spiritual crossing of the Jordan in baptism can receive no more important message from the life of Joshua than the need to develop a personal devotional life. All of us on the borders of heavenly Canaan must learn well the lesson of Joshua—to "rise early" for communion with God before undertaking the activities of the day.

Joshua 3:3 describes the next aspect of Israel's preparation for passage into Canaan: "And they [Joshua's officers] commanded the people, saying, 'When you see the ark of the covenant of the Lord your God, and the priests, the Levites, bearing it, then you shall set out from your place and go after it.'"

The showpiece of the story of the crossing of the Jordan is the ark of the covenant. The two chapters narrating this story mention the ark a total of 20 times! Israel was to focus upon the ark—the visible representation of the presence of God. With their eyes on the ark, whenever and wherever it went, they were to follow.

Here is a vital lesson for spiritual Israel! Not just in the morning, but all day long we must practice the presence of God. Where He leads, we follow. We make no moves, enter into no activity, unless with the eyes of faith we see the ark of God leading the way.

The ark not only symbolized God's presence, but presented the balanced picture of the gospel. Inside the ark rested the law of God, representing His standard of justice. Above the ark stood the bloodstained mercy seat (see Lev. 16:15, 16), coming between the immutable divine law and the Shekinah glory of God's presence enthroned upon the ark. Thus the eye of faith—penetrating beneath the blue cloth and badger skin and veil that covered the ark as it traveled (see Num. 4:5, 6)—could discern the beauty of the gospel, God's holy justice and judgment against sin combined with His mercy and forgiving grace based upon the substitutionary blood of Christ.

Ten times these two chapters refer to the ark as the "ark of the covenant" or the "ark of the covenant of the Lord." The ark is inextricably linked with the covenant the Lord made between Himself and His people. Entering into the Promised Land involved focusing upon the covenant—the Lord's promise to bless and empower His people as they respond in gratitude and covenant faithfulness.

The mention of the covenant in connection with the typology of baptism is significant inasmuch as baptism is entering into covenant relationship with God. "The Father, the Son, and the Holy Ghost, powers infinite and omniscient, receive those who truly enter into covenant relation with God. They are present at every baptism, to receive the candidates who have renounced the world and have received Christ into the soul temple" *(The SDA Bible Commentary*, Ellen G. White Comments, vol. 6, p. 1075). The covenant is mutual: "At our baptism we pledged ourselves to break all connection with Satan and his agencies, and to put heart and mind and soul into the work of extending the kingdom of God. All heaven is working for this object. The Father, the Son, and the Holy Spirit are pledged to cooperate with sanctified human instrumentalities" *(ibid.).* "The Father, the Son, and the Holy Spirit, the three holy dignitaries of heaven, have declared that They will strengthen men to overcome the powers of darkness. All the facilities of heaven are pledged to those who by their baptismal vows have entered into a covenant with God" *(ibid.,* vol. 5, p. 1110).

Soon, at the close of the great controversy, the Jordan typology will reach its consummation: the ark with its two tables of stone will again be the focus of the whole world as God brings it forth on the great judgment day *(ibid.,* vol. 1, p. 1109), the voice of God will deliver to His people the everlasting covenant *(The Great*

Controversy, pp. 640, 641),[4] and we will cross over literally, with God at our head, into heavenly Canaan.

Joshua 3:5 describes further preparation for crossing to Canaan: "And Joshua said to the people, 'Sanctify yourselves, for tomorrow the Lord will do wonders among you.'" This process of sanctification or consecration [Hebrew *qādaš*] involved the putting away of sin and removal of "all outward impurity" *(Patriarchs and Prophets*, p. 483).

We hear God's call to all those preparing for spiritual passage through the waters of baptism. Meditation and prayer and focusing upon God will reveal our sinfulness, and God will implant a desire to put away sin and consecrate ourselves to Him. All of us must daily reconsecrate ourselves to God and surrender all of our plans to Him, giving our lives into His hands each moment of each day (see *Steps to Christ*, p. 70). We will put away sin, not by trying harder in our own strength, but by trusting more fully in the power of God.

The Miracle

Visiting the Jordan River today, even in springtime, does not give a true picture of the mighty force of the river in Joshua's time, since now most of the water gets diverted for drinking and irrigation before it ever reaches the Jordan Valley. But in Joshua's day in the springtime, the Jordan "overflowed its banks," becoming a swollen and impetuous, "angry, surging stream," "impossible to cross at the usual fording places" *(Patriarchs and Prophets*, pp. 483, 484; cf. Joshua 3:15).

In exact fulfillment of God's prediction, as the feet of the priests carrying the ark dipped into the overflowing waters, "the waters which came down from upstream stood still, and rose up in a heap very far away at Adam" (Joshua 3:16), a city some 20 miles north of where Israel crossed.

The miracle may have occurred by God's direct suspension of the laws of nature, or just as miraculously by God working through His laws and providing the exact timing to accomplish His purposes. *The SDA Bible Commentary* suggests the latter possibility:

"The fact is, history records at least two instances during the past 700 years when the Jordan suddenly ceased flowing and many miles of the river bed remained dry for a number of hours. As a result of an earthquake, on the night preceding December 8, 1267, a large section of the west bank opposite Damieh fell into the river, completely damming its flow for 16 hours. . . . [At Damieh,] the Biblical city of Adam [Adamah], not far from where the Jabbok flows into the Jordan, the river valley narrows into a gorge that makes such an occurrence as the complete blocking of the river a comparatively simple matter.

"On July 11, 1927, the river ran dry again. A landslide near the ford at Tell ed-Damiyeh, caused by a severe earthquake, carried away part of the west bank of the river, thus blocking its flow for 21 hours and flooding much of the plain around Tell ed-Damiyeh. . . .

"We would ask: How could Joshua know a day ahead that an earthquake would block the river 20 miles upstream? Even more incredible, how could he know that exact moment of the earthquake, in order to direct the priests bearing the ark to march forward so that their feet would reach the riverbank just when the water ceased to flow?" *(The SDA Bible Commentary,* vol. 2, p. 41).[5]

Donald Madvig points out that "if an earthquake was responsible for stopping the Jordan River, it was still a miracle. The discovery of secondary causes only serves to explain how God did what He did, and only God's intervention can account for the miraculous timing."[6]

The miracle of the crossing showed God's might, that He is "the living God" who can be trusted for His continued presence with and protection of His people (see Joshua 3:10). It magnified Joshua before the people, as the crossing of the Red Sea had done for Moses 40 years before (verse 7). Finally, it increased the terror of the Canaanites for Israel and Israel's God (Joshua 5:1).

Though perhaps not always as outwardly dramatic as crossing the Jordan, every repentant, consecrated sinner passing through the waters of baptism constitutes just as great a miracle. A changed life shows God's might and trustworthiness. Every baptism magnifies the new Joshua and causes Satan's hosts to tremble. Likewise, our literal passage into heavenly Canaan will be accompanied by the song of the redeemed, heard by the entire universe: "Great and marvelous are Your works, Lord God Almighty! Just and true are Your ways, O King of the saints!" (Rev. 15:3). Ultimate glory will go to Jesus, the new Joshua, and ultimate terror and eventual destruction to Satan and his hosts.

The Memorials

As the Israelites crossed the Jordan, they erected two stone memorials, one of 12 stones in the midst of the Jordan (Joshua 4:9) and another 12-stoned memorial at Gilgal, their first campsite on the west bank of the Jordan. In the days ahead, as they returned from their battles during the conquest, the people could look at these memorials and be reminded of God's faithfulness. Also, in time to come, when later generations would see the memorials and ask their parents "What do these stones mean?" the parents would have opportunity to retell the story of the miraculous crossing of the Jordan.

On other occasions in Old Testament history God's people constructed stone monuments to commemorate something that had happened (see Gen. 28:18-22; 31:45-47; Joshua 24:26, 27). The closest parallel to the stone monuments of the Jordan crossing is Samuel's erecting of Ebenezer—"the stone of help"—after Israel's victory over the Philistines (1 Sam. 7:9-12).

As we stood on the site of ancient Ebenezer, my seminary students and I sang the second stanza of "Come, Thou Fount of Every Blessing," which has those poignant words: "Here I raise my Ebenezer, hither by Thy help I've come . . ." I thought then of the encouragement Ellen White gives for us to raise spiritual Ebenezers in the form of diary entries, as monuments of thankfulness to God. She asks the rhetorical question: "Brethren, where are the monuments by which you keep in view the love and goodness of God?" (*The SDA Bible Commentary*, Ellen G. White Comments, vol. 2, p. 1012).

Israel not only erected two stone monuments at the crossing of the Jordan but also had two "living memorials"—circumcision and the Passover. During the years of wilderness wandering after the rebellion at Kadesh Barnea, God suspended both ceremonies as a testimony of divine displeasure at their desire to return to Egypt. But now at Gilgal—which means "a rolling away" or "rolling off"—the years of wilderness wandering and rejection ended as God rolled away from them the reproach of Egypt (Joshua 5:9).

It seemed the very opposite of what wise military strategy would dictate—to virtually disable the whole army by circumcision and leave them vulnerable to an attack by the enemy, and then to delay an immediate attack in order to keep the Passover. But God knew that Israel's spiritual readiness was far more important than any human military advantage.

Circumcision was the outward sign of ethnic Israel's belonging to the covenant people of God, and the corresponding sign for spiritual Israel in New Testament times is baptism (Col. 2:11, 12). Baptism is thus not just a rite of passage into spiritual Canaan, but a joining up with God's covenant people, the church.

Likewise, Passover was the religious festival of Israel that pointed back to their redemption from Egyptian bondage by the blood of the paschal lamb, and forward to its antitype, the Lamb of God, who died at Passover time to redeem us from the bondage of sin. In the upper room, just before His death, Christ instituted the Lord's Supper as the New Testament memorial of His death (Matt. 26:26-29; 1 Cor. 11:23-26).

Thus spiritual Israel, like Israel of old, has two "living memorials" of their passage into spiritual Canaan: baptism and the Lord's Supper.

At the end of time when we literally pass into heavenly Canaan, both memorials will be consummated. John the revelator beholds the 144,000 standing on the sea of glass—the antitypical Red Sea/Jordan River—singing the song of Moses and the Lamb. No longer in need of cleansing from sin, they are not immersed in the water, but *standing* upon it—the symbol of victory and conquest (Rev. 15:1-4; see Joshua 10:24, 25). And the ultimate Passover/Lord's Supper will be celebrated in heaven at the marriage supper of the Lamb, when Jesus once again drinks of the fruit of the vine (see Matt. 26:29; Rev. 19:9).

"Friday, June 17, near sundown. My greatest personal monument to the crossing into Canaan occurred today. I am back in the U.S.A. at a Pathfinder backpacking trip in the wilderness area of south Manitou Island in northern Michigan. I have packed my notebook and during my free time have been in my tent putting the finishing touches on this chapter. My son, Jonathan, and his best friend, Kevin Lehmann, have just told me this afternoon that they would like to be baptized! There can be no greater 'living memorials' to this dad's heart than to have his only son and his son's best friend choose to spiritually cross over to Canaan through the waters of baptism. Here I raise my Ebenezer!"

---

[1] Our crossing went from Israel (west of the Jordan River) to Jordan (ancient Transjordan), and not from Transjordan to Canaan, as ancient Israel traveled. Yet the experience had many similarities to the obstacles incurred by ancient Israel.

[2] See George Balentine, "The Concept of the New Exodus in the Gospels" (unpublished Th.D. dissertation, Southern Baptist Theological Seminary, 1961), pp. 204-238, 283-286; and George Wesley Buchanan, *Typology and the Gospel* (Lanham, N.Y.: University Press of America, 1987), pp. 45-48, 64, 65, 87. In the antitypical flow of Matthew's gospel, Jesus, the New Israel, like the old, as God's Son, comes out of Egypt after a death decree (Matt. 2:14-16), has His "Red Sea" experience at the Jordan (Matt. 3), followed by 40 days in the wilderness, like ancient Israel's 40 years (Matt. 4). Then He gives the Sermon on the Mount, just as Moses repeated the law in Deuteronomy 40 years after the Exodus (Matt. 5-7).

[3] It appears that God intended these two experiences to go hand in hand—experientially understanding the gospel and being baptized—just as He originally desired that Israel cross the Red Sea and then head straight for the Promised Land without 40 years of wilderness wandering (see *Selected Messages,* book 1, p. 68). But just as ancient Israel made its detour before entering Canaan, so often Christians cross the Red Sea in baptism but do not experientially enter the "rest of grace" through faith until they have wandered long in a barren wilderness of unbelief and lack of power.

[4] God's voice delivers the everlasting covenant in its consummated fullness by glorifying His people (cf. *The Great Controversy,* pp. 640, 641 with p. 645: "At the voice of God they were glorified; now [at the Second Coming] they are made immortal and with the risen saints are caught up to meet their Lord in the air").

[5] For more details, see John Garstang and J.B.E. Garstang, *The Story of Jericho* (London: Marshall, Morgan, and Scott, 1948), pp. 136, 137.

[6] Madvig, "Joshua," p. 272.

The Shout
of Victory

6

Monday, April 25. From the top of Tell es-Sulṭân, ancient Jericho, I look out some two miles to the east of where I stand and some 600 feet lower in elevation, to the vicinity of ancient Gilgal, where Israel camped after crossing the Jordan. In my mind's eye I see Joshua rising early to meditate and pray, and meeting the pre-Incarnate Christ, his Commander.

"I imagine the thoughts of the people of Jericho as they watch the waters of the Jordan dry up for Israel to pass, then as they see Israel camped around the sanctuary at Gilgal, and again as they watch Israel's army marching around their city to the call of their rams' horn trumpets. I visualize their hearts melting in terror, with no longer any spirit in them because of Israel (Joshua 5:1), yet unwilling to renounce their debasing idolatry and acknowledge Yahweh as the true and living God.

"Then I imagine the horror of Jericho's inhabitants as a mighty shout follows the sevenfold circuit on the seventh day, and the walls come tumbling down. Finally, I relive the joy of Israel after that shout of victory and the conquest and destruction of the city. . . ."

"Joshua fit de battle of Jericho, Jericho, Jericho! Joshua fit de battle of Jericho, and de walls came a'tumblin' down." The action-packed story found in Joshua 6 inspired this powerful African-American spiritual, and still continues to enthrall readers with its battle drama.

The Modern Battle of Jericho

But the battle of Jericho did not end when Israel conquered and destroyed the city that spring day in 1410 B.C. For the "battle of Jericho" continues unabated in scholarly circles to this day. Today it rages over whether such a battle at Jericho ever happened at all![1] Most modern critical biblical scholars do not believe Jericho was even inhabited at the time purported in the Bible story, let alone there being an actual battle taking place as described in the biblical narrative.

Already in the early 1900s, when the German scholars Ernst Sellin and Carl Watzinger (1907-1909, 1911) undertook the first major excavation, they concluded that the site of Jericho was unoccupied during the entire Late Bronze Period (1550-1200 B.C.), and therefore no battle like the one described in the Bible could have occurred there.

British archaeologist John Garstang questioned their interpretation and mounted his own excavation at the site from 1930-1936. Garstang came to a far different conclusion:

"In a word, in all material details and in date the fall of Jericho took place as described in the biblical narrative. Our demonstration is limited, however, to material observations: the walls fell, shaken apparently by earthquake, and the city was destroyed by fire, about 1400 B.C. These are the basic facts resulting from our investigations. The link with Joshua and the Israelites is only circumstantial, but it seems to be solid and without a flaw."[2]

Some of his colleagues rejected Garstang's findings, and finally in the 1950s another British archaeologist, Kathleen Kenyon, conducted further archaeological excavations at the site (1952-1958). Her conclusions resembled those of Sellin and Watzinger earlier in the century: Jericho was destroyed about 1550 B.C. and remained unoccupied at the time the biblical record claimed for its destruction. No city of Jericho existed in Joshua's time for Israel to conquer!

Kenyon's work carried the day among many scholars, and indeed they still use it as a prime example of how the findings of modern archaeology contradict and even disprove the biblical record. It has become a benchmark piece of evidence to show that the Israelite conquest of Canaan claimed by Scripture never really took place. Many critical scholars tend to regard those who still accept the historicity of the biblical account of the conquest as naive and unscientific.

Recent "Shaking of the Walls"

But recent developments are rattling the critical scholars' consensus! Since the posthumous publication of Kenyon's final excavation reports some 30 years after the excavations and 12 years after her death, Bryant Wood, an authority in Canaanite Late Bronze Age pottery, has reanalyzed all of the available archaeological data from excavations at Jericho. His electrifying scholarly papers[3] and articles[4] have sent shock waves throughout the community of critical biblical archaeologists. I was personally present at one of his presentations at a prestigious scholarly society annual meeting and felt the "electricity" in the air as the implications of his work became apparent to the critical scholars in attendance.

Support for Biblical Chronology of Jericho

Bryant Wood has shown that Kathleen Kenyon, despite her meticulous fieldwork and detailed reporting of excavation results, had serious flaws in her analysis of data and her dating methodology. As she sought to establish the chronology of the city, she based her analysis of pottery types[5] on what was *not* found rather than on what *was* found. Since she found none of the bichrome (red-and-black painted) ware pottery imported from Cyprus, common to the Late Bronze I period (1550-1400 B.C.), she concluded that the city had been destroyed before 1550 B.C.

Unfortunately she failed to recognize that she had dug in a small excavation area (two 8 x 8 meter squares) in the poorer part of the city, where we would not expect to find such exotic ware. She also failed to note the numerous examples of domestic pottery that can be dated to the late Late Bronze I period (about 1400 B.C.), the very time of the Israelite conquest, according to Scripture. Further, she overlooked the fact that Garstang had found a considerable quantity of the imported Cypriot bichrome ware as he dug in the rich palace area of the tell. In a word, contrary to Kenyon's conclusions but according to evidence in her own field reports that she paid no attention to, pottery chronology supports the biblical record precisely!

Besides the evidence from pottery chronology, Wood sets forth three additional lines of evidence supporting the chronological accuracy of the biblical account. First, Garstang found a whole series of scarabs (inscribed Egyptian amulets in the shape of a sacred dung beetle) in the Jericho cemetery northwest of the city that we can date right up to the end of the Late Bronze I period, or about 1400 B.C., the time of the conquest. Obviously the cemetery was in continuous use during the time Kenyon claimed the city was unoccupied!

Second, Kenyon found 20 different architectural phases at the tell, starting from about 1650 B.C. If the city had undergone destruction in 1550 B.C., then all 20 phases would have to have been squeezed into a short 100-year period, which is highly unlikely. But adding another 150 years would give ample time for such phases.

Finally, a carbon-14 sample taken from a piece of charcoal found in the destruction layer of the city dated to 1410 B.C.—the very year indicated by biblical chronology for the fall of Jericho!

Thus, contrary to Kenyon and the modern critical consensus, people did indeed live in the Old Testament city of Jericho at the time of Joshua, and it was destroyed at the very time Scripture indicates.

Jericho in Scripture and Archaeology

Bryant Wood's study not only supported the chronology of Scripture regarding the fall of Jericho, but indicates extraordinary correlations between details of the biblical record and archaeological data. Here is a summary of the major points:

1. The city was strongly fortified (Joshua 2:5, 7, 15; 6:5, 20). Archaeological evidence reveals two walls. A lower stone revetment wall stood some 15 feet high at the base of the tell. On top of it rose a mud-brick parapet wall that archaeologists found preserved at one point to a height of eight feet. The stone revetment wall held in place a huge earth-packed glacis, or embankment. At the top of the embankment was the upper mud-brick wall, probably some 6.5 feet thick and 12 feet high.

2. Evidence revealed many houses like that of Rahab, located between the lower revetment/parapet and upper wall, thus literally

"in the wall" (Joshua 2:15, RSV).

3. Many jars filled with grain occupied the ground-floor rooms of the destruction debris. Finding such large quantities of stored grain is almost unheard-of in Palestinian excavations. It implies that the city was attacked in the springtime just after harvest, exactly as the biblical account indicates (Joshua 2:6; 3:15; 5:10).

4. The stores of grain also reveal that the inhabitants had no opportunity to flee with their foodstuffs; again as the Bible records: "Now Jericho was securely shut up because of the children of Israel; none went out, and none came in" (Joshua 6:1).

5. The large quantities of grain also suggest that the siege was short, unlike most sieges in ancient Near Eastern warfare. Again this agrees with the biblical account of only a seven-day siege (verse 15).

6. A final implication of the huge amounts of grain found in the destruction debris is that nobody plundered the city. Armies that managed to capture a city would seize the valuable items, including the grain. But in the case of Jericho, this did not happen, in harmony with the biblical divine injunction to Israel, "Now the city shall be doomed by the Lord to destruction [Hebrew *ḥērem*], it and all who are in it. . . . And you, by all means keep yourselves from the accursed things *[ḥērem]*, lest you become accursed *[ḥērem]*" (verses 17, 18).

7. The walls of the city were leveled probably by a massive earthquake. Kenyon herself, although dating the destruction of the city too early, describes the collapse of the city walls and rooms prior to their destruction by fire. Again the biblical account rings true: "The wall fell down flat" (verse 20) by the divinely instigated quaking of the earth.

8. Archaeological investigations reveal that the mudbricks of the upper wall collapsed and tumbled down the steep plastered embankment between the two walls, and together with bricks from the collapsed lower parapet wall, deposited rubble at the base of the stone revetment wall. Kenyon describes finding "a heavy fill of fallen red [mud] bricks piling nearly to the top of the revetment [wall]. These [red bricks] probably came from the wall on the summit of the bank."[6] The fallen mud bricks from the walls formed rough ramps all around the city so that the biblical account

makes good sense: "the people [of Israel's army] *went up* into the city, *every man straight before him,* and they took the city" (verse 20). The Israelite soldiers were able to each move straight ahead, surmount the 15-foot-high stone revetment wall by climbing up over the filled-in rubble of the collapsed mud-brick walls, and then easily scale the earth-packed embankment and enter the city.

9. The city totally burned. Kathleen Kenyon describes the conflagration:

"The destruction was complete. Walls and floors were blackened or reddened by fire, and every room was filled with fallen bricks, timbers, and household utensils; in most rooms the fallen debris was heavily burnt, but the collapse of the walls of the eastern rooms seems to have taken place before they were affected by the fire."[7]

John Garstang describes the destruction by fire in graphic terms:

"The traces of fire upon its [the room's] walls were as fresh as though it had occurred a month before; each scrape of the trowel exposed a black layer of charcoal, where the roof had burned, or caused the piled up ashes to run down in a stream. On a brick ledge in a corner of this room we found the family provisions of dates, barley, oats, olives, an onion, and peppercorns, all charred but unmistakable; while a little store of bread, together with a quantity of unbaked dough which had been laid aside to serve as leaven for the morrow's baking, told plainly the same tale of a people cut off in full activity."[8]

Such a depiction fits the biblical narrative precisely. After the collapse of the walls and destruction of its inhabitants (except Rahab and her house), "they burned the city and all that was in it with fire" (verse 24).

10. Archaeological findings reveal that the site of Old Testament Jericho remained unoccupied following its destruction for several centuries throughout the Late Bronze Age (1400-1200 B.C.), except for a small residency-type building constructed toward the end of the fourteenth century but abandoned shortly thereafter. It was then reoccupied in the Iron Age after 1000 B.C. Again this correlates exactly with the biblical data.

Following Jericho's destruction, Joshua warned, "Cursed be the man before the Lord who rises up and builds this city Jericho;

he shall lay its foundation with his firstborn, and with his youngest he shall set up its gates" (verse 26). For hundreds of years the city lay in ruins except for the small residency built by Eglon, king of Moab, and inhabited by him for some 18 years till his assassination (Judges 3:14-30). The Iron Age reoccupancy correlates with an event from the time of King Ahab (874-853 B.C.), recorded in 1 Kings 16:34: "In his [King Ahab's] days Hiel of Bethel built Jericho. He laid its foundation with [margin: at the cost of the life of] Abiram his firstborn, and with his youngest son Segub he set up its gates, according to the word of the Lord, which He had spoken through Joshua the son of Nun."

The Battle Continues

The modern "battle of Jericho" is not over. Despite Bryant Wood's penetrating reanalysis of the data, skeptics still abound. Ironically, although they cannot repudiate his interpretation of the basic data, many critical scholars refuse to accept his conclusion of a literal destruction of Jericho c. 1400 B.C. by Israel, because, they say, there is no evidence of Israel's conquest at this time! We call this kind of thinking circular reasoning! Evidence is used to establish a point and then the point is employed to establish the evidence. Kenyon's conclusions regarding Jericho had long been the showcase evidence against a literal conquest c. 1400 B.C., and now many scholars use the rejection of a literal conquest c. 1400 B.C. to deny Wood's conclusions regarding Jericho!

I have spent so much space in this chapter recounting the modern discussions on Jericho not only to provide illumination and confirmation of the biblical account but also because the basic issue in the modern "battle" is the same issue that Joshua and the people of Israel had to face at the historical battle of Jericho.

The plan that God gave Joshua for taking the city did not make any sense in normal military strategy. From a human point of view, God's command seemed like a foolhardy procedure. Against the seemingly impregnable fortifications of the city, fighting with rams' horns, silence, and shouts? Furthermore, only Joshua personally received God's command. The people did not see or hear the "Captain of the Lord's host." They had to take their leader's word for it and by faith follow his commands, even if they did not seem to make any sense to human wisdom.

The question echoes down from the battle of Jericho:

"Would those who today profess to be God's people conduct themselves thus under similar circumstances? Doubtless many would wish to follow out their own plans and would suggest other ways and means of accomplishing the desired end. They would be loath to submit to so simple an arrangement and one that reflected upon themselves no glory, save the merit of obedience. They would also question the possibility of a mighty city being conquered in that manner. But the law of duty is supreme. It should hold sway over human reason. Faith is the living power that presses through every barrier, overrides all obstacles, and plants its banner in the heart of the enemy's camp" *(Testimonies,* vol. 4, p. 163).

The modern "battle of Jericho," among critical scholars—and among all of us as Christians—boils down to the same issue as long ago: Are we willing to take God at His word, to do as He says because we trust Him even though it does not always make sense to our human reason? In a thousand different areas of doctrine and lifestyle, the modern scenario is: "God says, but I think . . ."[9] Will we learn what the people of Israel experienced at Jericho, to take God at His word and let the law of duty hold sway over human reason or feeling?

Spiritual Israel, hear the word of the Lord, hear the message of Jericho, hear the battle plan for our spiritual warfare: "God works mightily for a faithful people who obey His word without questioning or doubt" *(ibid.,* p. 164). Let us walk in the spiritual footsteps of Joshua and Israel at our battles of Jericho today!

---

[1] For this overview of the history of archaeological investigation of Old Testament Jericho, I am indebted to Bryant G. Wood, who wrote the illuminating article "Did the Israelites Conquer Jericho? A New Look at the Archaeological Evidence," *Biblical Archaeology Review,* March/April 1990, pp. 45-57.

[2] John Garstang, "Jericho and the Biblical Story," in *Wonders of the Past,* ed. J. A. Hammerton (New York: Wise, 1937), p. 122, cited in Wood, p. 49.

[3] For example, his paper presented at Andrews University, Jan. 28, 1988, entitled "Uncovering the Truth at Jericho: A Comparison of the Archaeological and Biblical History of Jericho in the Late Bronze Age."

[4] See especially his article in the 1990 *Biblical Archaeology Review* cited earlier and his reply to critics, "Dating Jericho's Destruction: Bienkowski Is Wrong on All Counts," *Biblical Archaeology Review,* September/October 1990,

pp. 45, 47-49, 68, 69.

[5] In modern archaeological methods, pottery experts can establish a relative chronology of the different stratigraphic layers on the tell based upon the types of pottery found in those layers. This method rests upon two principles. First, the fundamental principle of stratigraphy: since every successive occupation of a site is built on top of the previous ruins, each undisturbed higher stratigraphic layer on the tell represents a later period than the one below it. Second, the basic principle of pottery typology: each chronological period has pottery with characteristics unique to that period.

[6] Kathleen Kenyon, *Excavations at Jericho: The Architecture and Stratigraphy of the Tell (Jericho 3),* ed. Thomas A. Holland (London: BSAJ, 1981), p. 370, cited in Wood, p. 54.

[7] Cited in Wood, p. 56.

[8] John Garstang and J.B.E. Garstang, *The Story of Jericho* (London: Marshall, Morgan, and Scott, 1948), p. 141.

[9] See the development of this theme with current examples in Morris Venden, *God Says, But I Think* (Boise, Idaho: Pacific Press, 1993).

Treachery
in the Camp

7

Friday, May 6, early morning. We turn off the main road from Jericho to Jerusalem onto a narrow road unfrequented by tourists. Our VW van winds its way up through the rolling barren foothills of the Wilderness of Judea, just a few miles west of the cliffs behind Qumran. The road rises in elevation from some 1,000 feet below sea level in the Jordan Valley to about sea level, and the narrow winding route opens out into a level valley isolated among the surrounding wilderness mountains. We are now in the plain el-Buqeah, called in Joshua's day the Valley of Achor, the Valley of Trouble. . . .

"I visualize Joshua, early in the morning, leading Achan and his family up the some 1,000-foot elevation from Gilgal [see Joshua 7:24: "Joshua then took Achan son of Zerah and *led him up* to the Vale of Achor" New Jerusalem], some 10 miles through the rugged and barren wilderness, to this isolated valley. There is plenty of room for all Israel to assemble. The valley floor is about two miles wide and five miles long. Israeli military tents now pitched at one end of the valley for an army bivouac remind me of the Israelite soldiers who lost their lives in the battle of Ai because of Achan's sin, and I recall the stolen gold, silver, and garment hidden under Achan's tent.

"In my imagination I see the place of execution, witness the stoning, the burning, the erection of the great heap of stones over the 'troubler of Israel.' An isolated wilderness valley becomes the Valley of Trouble. . . ."

Reasons for the Reversal

Up to this point in the book of Joshua, the story has been one of unqualified success. But now Israel is in full retreat, defeated by the enemy. Joshua falls on his face before God, filled with anguish and agony. The omnipotent character of Israel's God has been maligned before the onlooking Canaanites.

What caused the setback? Certainly God had not purposed Israel's failure and defeat. He had made provision for uninterrupted victory. Three reasons for Israel's failure emerge from the biblical account, reasons that lie at the root of our own setbacks and failures in the Christian warfare.

First, Israel became self-confident after the battle of Jericho. At Jericho God had planned the battle using such simple and unlikely means so that Israel could not take the glory to themselves (see the *SDA Bible Commentary*, Ellen G. White Comments, vol. 2, p. 995). Yet even though they had not won by their own brilliant strategy or great military power, but solely by God's supernatural intervention in casting down the walls, nonetheless they became self-confident. They "failed to realize that divine help alone could give them success" *(Patriarchs and Prophets, p. 493)*. We face the same tendency and danger today after some great spiritual victory of our own.

Second, there was a lack of prayer. Self-confidence led even Joshua to make plans for the conquest of Ai without seeking counsel from God (see Joshua 7:2, 3; *Patriarchs and Prophets,* pp. 493, 494). In the flush of victory at Jericho, he didn't go back to Gilgal, to his quiet place of communion with his heavenly Commander. Instead, he sent scouts and then the 3,000 soldiers, straight from Jericho to Ai. If he had sought the Lord for directions, he would have learned of the sin in the camp and would never have been humbled in the dust by the defeat at Ai. So today, how often in the flush of spiritual victory have we failed to pray, trusting to ourselves rather than bowing in humility and thanksgiving before the One who gave the victory?

The third cause of defeat for Israel was disobedience. God told Joshua as he lay prostrate on the ground: "Get up! Why do you lie thus on your face? Israel has sinned, and they have also transgressed My covenant which I commanded them. For they have even taken some of the accursed [devoted, Hebrew *ḥērem*] things, and have both stolen and deceived; and they have also put it among their own stuff" (Joshua 7:10, 11). The Lord explained to Israel's military leader that because of this sin in the camp, Israel had met defeat and the divine presence could not be with Israel until it had dealt with the sin.

Achan's Sin

Already at the beginning of the Ai-Achan narrative, in Joshua 7:1, Scripture informs us of the nature of the sin: Israel had "committed a trespass" [Hebrew *māʿal*, "acted undercover, underhandedly, treacherously, unfaithfully"] in regard to the *ḥērem*, the things devoted to God for destruction or sacred use, for Achan had taken from these devoted things. Verse 11 indicates that it involved transgression of the divine covenant, stealing, and deceit. Achan's own confession is even more specific: "When I saw among the spoils a beautiful Babylonian garment, two hundred shekels of silver, and a wedge of gold weighing fifty shekels, I coveted them and took them. And there they are, hidden in the earth in the midst of my tent, with the silver under it" (verse 21).

Achan's root sin was that of covetousness. It was behind the very first sin in the universe (Isa. 14:13, 14), as well as the first sin of Israel upon entering Canaan (Joshua 7), and the first recorded sin in the New Testament church (Acts 5:1-11). The sin of covetousness is especially offensive to God (see Matt. 6:24; Luke 12:15; Eph. 5:3; Col. 3:5; *Patriarchs and Prophets*, pp. 496, 497). The tenth commandment of the Decalogue forbidding coveting is essentially different than the other nine because it "strikes at the very root of all sins, prohibiting the selfish desire, from which springs the sinful act" (*ibid.*, p. 309). It was this commandment that exposed the apostle Paul to his deep-rooted sinfulness (Rom. 7:7, 14, 25), when before this he had boasted of his righteousness (Phil. 3:4-6).

Covetousness is like a "deadly leprosy" (*The SDA Bible Commentary*, Ellen G. White Comments, vol. 2, p. 996) that slowly infects the life. Ellen White describes its insidious course of infection:

"Covetousness is an evil of gradual development. Achan had

cherished greed of gain until it became a habit, binding him in fetters well-nigh impossible to break. While fostering this evil, he would have been filled with horror at the thought of bringing disaster upon Israel; but his perceptions were deadened by sin, and when temptation came, he fell an easy prey" *(Patriarchs and Prophets,* p. 496).

Its corrupting influence goes beyond the individual. "One man infected with its deadly leprosy may communicate the taint to thousands" *(The SDA Bible Commentary,* Ellen G. White Comments, vol. 2, p. 996).

The sin of covetousness abounds today as well. "Everywhere its slimy track is seen. . . . And this evil exists not in the world alone, but in the church. How common even here to find selfishness, avarice, overreaching, neglect of charities, and robbery of God 'in tithes and offerings'" *(Patriarchs and Prophets,* p. 497). When Ellen White penned volume 5 of the *Testimonies for the Church,* she could write that "every church and almost every family has its Achan" (p. 157). Is it any better today?

It should be pointed out that covetousness refers to far more than selfish desire for material possessions. In particular, note that the tenth commandment also forbids coveting one's neighbor's wife. The word for "covet" in the tenth commandment and in the Joshua narrative is *ḥāmad,* and this same word is translated "lust" in the counsel against immorality: "Do not lust *[ḥāmad]* after her [the immoral woman's] beauty in your heart" (Prov. 6:25; see also *Testimonies to Ministers and Gospel Workers,* p. 428, for the connection of the Achan story with the sin of fornication).

Israel's Sin

So far we have looked at Achan's individual sin. But the biblical text is clear that Israel as a nation was also corporately guilty: "*Israel* has sinned, and *they* have also transgressed My covenant" (Joshua 7:11). Ellen White underscores the corporate responsibility for Achan's sin: "the nation was held accountable for the guilt of the transgressor" *(Patriarchs and Prophets,* p. 494). "Achan's sin brought disaster upon the whole nation. For one man's sin the displeasure of God will rest upon His church till the transgression is searched out and put away" *(ibid.,* p. 497). Still again, "God holds His people, as a body, responsible for the sins existing in individuals among them" *(Testimonies,* vol. 3, p. 269).

Dealing With Sin: Abiding Principles

The way Joshua promptly dealt with secret sin in the camp of Israel clearly indicates what the church should do in similar circumstances today. We must search out and put it away. But we note that God did not point out the offender immediately in order that each member of the congregation "might feel their responsibility for the sins existing among them, and thus be led to searching of heart and humiliation before God" *(Patriarchs and Prophets,* pp. 494, 495). This principle still applies to each church member:

"When the church is in difficulty, when coldness and spiritual declension exist, giving occasion for the enemies of God to triumph, then, instead of folding their hands and lamenting their unhappy state, let its members inquire if there is not an Achan in the camp. With humiliation and searching of heart, let each seek to discover the hidden sins that shut out God's presence" *(ibid.,* p. 497).

Achan could have confessed his sin in true penitence and been saved, but he resisted the promptings of conscience until it was too late, until only public exposure forced it from his hardened heart (see *ibid.,* pp. 497, 498). Inspiration draws back the curtain and poignantly portrays his feelings and actions as the public investigation proceeds:

"While he is rejoicing in his ill-gotten gain, his security is broken in upon; he hears that an investigation is to be made. This makes him uneasy. He repeats over and over to himself: What does it concern them? I am accountable for my acts. He apparently puts on a brave face and in the most demonstrative manner condemns the one guilty. If he had confessed he might have been saved; but sin hardens the heart, and he continues to assert his innocence. Amid so large a crowd he thinks he will escape detection. Lots are cast to search out the offender; the lot falls upon the tribe of Judah. Achan's heart now begins to throb with guilty fear, for he is one of that tribe; but still he flatters himself that he will escape. The lot is again cast, and the family to which he belongs is taken. Now in his pallid face his guilt is read by Joshua. The lot cast again singles out the unhappy man. There he stands, pointed out by the finger of God as the guilty one who has caused all this trouble" *(Testimonies,* vol. 4, p. 492).

Achan's admission of guilt when it was too late will be repeated on a worldwide scale by the guilty in the final judgment.

Along with the individual responsibility of each church member to search his own heart, church leaders have the duty to deal with sin in the church body: "If the leaders of the church neglect to diligently search out the sins which bring the displeasure of God upon the body, they become responsible for these sins" *(ibid.,* vol. 3, p. 269).

Though the example of Joshua and the above inspired counsel is true, it can be abused. Ardent reformers in the church whose overriding harsh spirit makes them unfit for this type of work, often seize upon it for their own ends. Immediately after the sentence from the pen of inspiration cited above, we read: "But to deal with minds is the nicest work in which men ever engaged. All are not fitted to correct the erring. They have not wisdom to deal justly, while loving mercy. They are not inclined to see the necessity of mingling love and tender compassion with faithful reproofs. Some are ever needlessly severe" *(ibid.,* pp. 269, 270).

On the other hand, some are too lenient and would object to doing anything about sin in the church. Ellen White also addresses this extreme in the next breath: "Should a case like Achan's be among us, there are many who would accuse those who might act the part of Joshua in searching out the wrong, of having a wicked, fault-finding spirit" *(ibid.,* p. 270). Elsewhere she writes: "There are many in this day that would designate Achan's sin as of little consequence, and would excuse his guilt; but it is because they have no realization of the character of sin and its consequences, no sense of the holiness of God and of His requirements" *(The SDA Bible Commentary,* Ellen G. White Comments, vol. 2, p. 998).

May God help us to find the balanced path of Joshua in dealing with sin in the camp, showing "tender compassion" (note how he addresses Achan as "my son," Joshua 7:19) combined with "faithful reproofs."

Some have been particularly concerned with the fact that Israel not only put Achan but his whole family to death at the Valley of Achor. Because he had buried the stolen goods in the family tent, we can assume that the whole family was involved in the sin and its coverup. Again the insights of Ellen White reveal explicitly what is only implicit in the text:

"Achan's parents had educated their son in such a way that he felt free to disobey the Word of the Lord, the principles inculcated in his life led him to deal with his children in such a way that they also were corrupted. Mind acts and reacts upon mind, and the punishment which included the relations of Achan with himself, reveals the fact that all were involved in the transgression *(ibid.)*.

Trouble Valley Becomes a Door of Hope

The life of Achan, the "troubler of Israel" (1 Chron. 2:7), ended in the Valley of Achor, the Valley of Trouble, but that is not the end of the story for the Valley of Achor. The later prophet Hosea utilized Israel's experience at Achor to illustrate the larger message of salvation. Though Israel as a nation in her later history was unfaithful to her Husband, Yahweh promised to have mercy on her and give her "the Valley of Achor as a door of hope" (Hosea 2:15).

Already in the book of Joshua, the Valley of Achor turned into a door of hope. Joshua and Israel learned their lesson about self-confidence and neglect of prayer, and they put away the sin in their midst. This led to God's signal blessing in the second battle of Ai that soon followed. Combining wise military strategy of ambush with divine power, Israel totally defeated and destroyed the inhabitants of Ai and burned the city.

Renew the Covenant!

In the flush of this victory it would seem militarily wise for Israel to press forward in the conquest of Canaan. But a more important work must take priority, the spiritual duty of renewing their covenant loyalty to God at Shechem, in fulfillment of God's instruction to Moses (see Deut. 11:29; 27; 28).

"Sunday, April 24. I sit here on top of Mount Gerizim, just before sundown. Just as Israel of old came through dangerous territory of unconquered foes but God supernaturally protected them, so we who have come to Mount Gerizim felt that God had protected us from harm. Our bus driver refused to bring us into the central hill country of Ephraim because of the danger of stonings and car bombings from both militant Israeli settlers and Arab Palestinian extremists. We finally found specially tagged Arab taxis, offered many prayers, and arrived safely atop Mount Gerizim, one of the highest mountains of central Palestine (2,891 feet).

"The view is spectacular, looking down to the vale of Shechem, more than 1,000 feet below, and up to Mount Ebal (3,084 feet) just to the north of the valley. I recall the inspired description of this site in Joshua's day that magnificently and accurately captured what I now see, far beyond my own powers of description:

" 'The spot chosen [Shechem] was one of the most beautiful in all Palestine, and worthy to be the theater where this grand and impressive scene was to be enacted. The lovely valley, its green fields dotted with olive groves, watered with brooks from living fountains, and gemmed with wildflowers, spread out invitingly between the barren hills. Ebal and Gerizim, upon opposite sides of the valley, nearly approach each other, their lower spurs seeming to form a natural pulpit, every word spoken on one being distinctly audible on the other, while the mountainsides, receding, afford space for a vast assemblage' *(Patriarchs and Prophets,* p. 500).

"I imagine Joshua erecting the stone monument on barren Mount Ebal, across the valley from where I sit, and inscribing the law upon the great plastered stones. In my mind's eye I see him erect the altar of uncut stones and offer burnt offerings there on the same steep and rocky mountain, Ebal, the Mountain of Curses, and I think how Jesus, the Lamb of God, died to take the curses I deserve (see Gal. 3:13; *Patriarchs and Prophets,* p. 500). . . . This thought takes on even more potency as now, a half hour later, after sundown on this Passover eve on top of Mount Gerizim, I watch the Samaritans sacrifice their Passover lambs. I'm revolted at seeing healthy innocent lambs, earlier frisking about and being ridden by the children who owned them, now having their throats slashed with the knife, some struggling, then falling helplessly to the ground. But the gruesome sight helps me visualize what happened on Mount Ebal in Joshua's day, and even more, what happened on Mount Calvary—for me!

"On windswept Mount Gerizim I also imagine the people of Israel reciting the blessings and curses as part of the sacred ceremony of covenant renewal. I too renew my covenant with the Lord on Mount Gerizim, the Mountain of Blessing. I claim the blessings of God that Israel repeated from Deuteronomy 28:1-14 and choose to be a faithful member of God's covenant people."

Will you also, in imagination, go to Mount Gerizim just now and join Israel in renewing your covenant vows before God?

Enemy Stratagem

8

Sabbath, May 28, just before sundown. Today is my last day in the Middle East. Early tomorrow morning I fly back to the States. As the last place to visit in the environs of Jerusalem, I choose Mount Nebĭ-Samwîl, the highest mountain (2,095 feet) surrounding Jerusalem and, according to tradition, the burial place of the prophet Samuel. The Crusaders called it Mons Gaudii (Mountain of Joy), because after coming on the road through the central mountain range from Joppa, they had their first glimpse of Jerusalem from its summit.

"From the dizzying height of the mosque minaret atop the mountain, in the clearness before evening, I too enjoy a spectacular panoramic view of Jerusalem, the modern city, its sprawling suburbs to the south and east reaching almost to the foot of the mountain. Some five or six miles to the southeast huddles the Old City, with the gray dome of the Church of the Holy Sepulchre and the gleaming golden Dome of the Rock. On the distant horizon the 200-foot tower of the Ascension Monastery on the Mount of Olives thrusts up against the sky.

"From the commanding height of Nebĭ-Samwîl, looking west, I can see much of the land inhabited by the enemy coalition described in Joshua 9:1. I can see the 'hill country' [NIV], the central mountains of Palestine. Farther west are the 'lowland' or 'western foothills' [NIV; Hebrew *Shephelah*], and beyond that the coasts of the 'Great Sea,' the plains of Philistia and Sharon, between the Mediterranean Sea and the Shephelah.

ENEMY STRATAGEM

"Those who are with me on the tower atop Nebī-Samwîl naturally fix their gaze upon the dazzling sights of Jerusalem to the south and east, and then look to the west, where on the distant horizon the setting sun lights up the Mediterranean Sea into a sea of gold . . . , and they completely overlook the beautiful valley to the north. I invite them to come to the northern railing of the mosque tower and look down. In the middle of the broad valley or basin before us, nestled among the green fields and surrounding hills, we see a steep round hill, with strikingly defined, horizontally stratified layers or bands of limestone rock formations. On this hill is the modern Arab village of el-Jîb, . . . and the excavated ruins of ancient Gibeon.

"Last week I visited the village of el-Jîb and the remains of ancient Gibeon with another group of students. Few tourists now come to this village because of the tension between Arab residents and nearby Jewish settlements, but we mustered our courage and drove through the village to the top of the tell, waving and shouting, *'Assalamu 'alaykum'* ['Peace be to you'] to all we met.

"At the archaeological excavations local Arab children gladly volunteered to take us down into the ancient circular well shaft, more than 80 feet deep and almost 40 feet in diameter, with an impressive winding staircase of 79 steps leading to the bottom. In the debris of this shaft archaeologists found 31 jar handles inscribed with the name 'Gibeon' [*gbᵓn* in ancient Hebrew script]. The children also led us through the sloping underground tunnel that runs from the well shaft to the groundwater chamber that was the source of water for the city. Because of the elaborate water system, the groundwater chamber outside of the walls of the city was accessible even during time of siege.[1]

"Before leaving the site we also were given a tour of the local museum of ancient artifacts, run by the grandmother of one of our self-appointed boy guides. As we left the tell I thought again of the ancient Gibeonites, who also left the tell, their town, but on quite a different mission. . . ."

A mission of deceptive subterfuge. We find these Hivites from Gibeon some three days later in the camp of Israel at Gilgal. With moldy bread, torn wineskins, old and patched sandals and garments, they claim to be ambassadors come on a long journey from far away, seeking a covenant of peace. Their ruse deceives Joshua and the people of Israel.

Modern "Gibeonite Strategy"

The Gibeonite strategy is one of Satan's favorite tactics against God's people. When a frontal attack will not work, he gains his ends by insidious internal subterfuge. Satan sows the tares among the wheat, and they are so like the true grain that their presence is apparent only when the grain ripens (see Matt. 13:24-30).

My wife just called my attention to an issue of *Christianity Today* that has a feature article describing the international feminist conference named RE-Imagining, sponsored by the Minnesota Council of Churches. The organizers of RE-Imagining called the conference "the dawn of a feminist reformation, a 'second reformation . . . much more basic and important to the health of humankind than the first.'" Throughout the conference presenters used Christian terminology but subtly filled it with new meaning, borrowed heavily from the New Age movement.

"The central task of conference participants was to 're-imagine God.' There was little room for the triune God of Christianity. In fact, Lutheran pastor Barbara Lundblad drew whoops and applause when she noted with satisfaction that 'we have done nothing in the name of the Father, and of the Son, and of the Holy Spirit.' Like several other speakers, 'womanist' theologian Delores Williams scoffed at the idea of Christ's atonement. 'I don't think we need folks hanging on crosses and blood dripping and weird stuff. . . . We just need to listen to the god within.'

"The deity of re-imagining was Sophia, nominally the biblical spirit of wisdom. Sophia, conference participants were told, is 'the suppressed part of the biblical tradition, and clearly the female face of the human psyche.' Prayers to Sophia named her as 'our maker, creator god, mother, and guide.' At the conference grand finale— the 'Struggle for Transformation Ritual'—participants worshiped Sophia in a rousing service complete with milk and honey."[2]

Here is just one of thousands of modern examples that we could cite of how Satan is introducing the tenets of spiritualism and other anti-Christian sentiments from within in his mission of deceptive subterfuge. The Christian church is making *shalom* [peace] with the enemies of God without realizing it. And the Seventh-day Adventist Church membership has not escaped the trend. Both as a corporate body facing wolves in "sheep's clothing" (Matt. 7:15) and in our individual encounter with the "deceitfulness of sin" (Heb. 3:13), Satan would destroy the church by deception from within.

How Not to Be Fooled

What was the cause of Israel's failure to recognize the insidious Gibeonite strategy? Israel repeated the same error as after the battle of Jericho: "They did not ask counsel of the Lord" (Joshua 9:14). Without divine eyesight to recognize the subterfuge, Joshua unknowingly made *shalom* with his enemies, the enemies of God. Only three days later did they find that they had been deceived. And by then it was too late to turn back.

This story is one of the most dramatic examples of the danger of trusting one's own judgment and "walking by sight." It is *never* safe to trust our own common sense without praying to God for guidance and wisdom. "There is a way which seems right to a man, but its end is the way of death" (Prov. 14:12; cf. Prov. 16:25). "Trust in the Lord with all your heart, and lean not on your own understanding; in all your ways acknowledge Him, and He shall direct your paths" (Prov. 3:5, 6). Especially in the matter of making alliances, we need the Lord's direction. To be "unequally yoked with unbelievers" is too often fatal to Christians in their spiritual warfare.

In the great tribulation of the last days, every evidence of our senses will cry out for us to "make *shalom*" with the enemies of God. The path of truth and error will lie so closely together that it will be impossible for us to distinguish one from the other unless we seek the "counsel of the Lord" in the Scriptures and through agonizing prayer. We will have to walk by faith when the evidences of our sight will seem to contradict what we know to be true from God's Word. Oh, that we might now learn from Joshua's failure and continually walk by faith and not by sight!

Lessons From Gibeon

The Gibeon narrative is also an important example of remaining true to one's word, even at the prospect of personal loss. Israel's covenant of peace with the Gibeonites had not violated the divine command to destroy the idolatrous Canaanites, since the Gibeonites had promised to renounce their idolatry and serve the Lord (see *Patriarchs and Prophets*, p. 506). Thus Israel had no legitimate reason to dissolve its oath to let the Gibeonites live. We need to follow the basic principle that is to characterize the Christian: "He who swears to his own hurt and does not change" (Ps. 15:4).

Like the story of Rahab, the Gibeon incident is also a great example of God's willingness and desire for the "salvation of the heathen." In the chapter of *Prophets and Kings* entitled "Hope for the Heathen," Ellen White writes: "The advancing hosts of Israel found that knowledge of the mighty workings of the God of the Hebrews had gone before them, and that some among the heathen were learning that He alone was the true God. . . . In the midst of the land a numerous people—the Gibeonites—renounced their heathenism and united with Israel, sharing in the blessings of the covenant" (p. 369).

Rahab was a harlot. Both she and the Gibeonites were liars. The Gibeonites dealt in deception apparently without a twinge of conscience. But like Rahab, even in the midst of their idolatry and moral flaws, they had heard of the mighty acts of Israel's God, Yahweh, and they told Joshua, "Your servants have come, because of the name [character] of the Lord your God; for we have heard of His fame, and all that He did in Egypt, and all that He did to the two kings of the Amorites who were beyond the Jordan" (Joshua 9:9, 10). Also, like Rahab, they were willing to leave their ties with their countrymen, to break with the confederacy of the Canaanites, and to join with God's people. And finally, like Rahab, the Gibeonites were brought into the midst of the people of Israel (see Joshua 10:1, which uses the same phrase *beqereb*, "in the midst," for the Gibeonites as for Rahab). And this leads to a final lesson of the narrative.

This account teaches that God can bring good out of even apparent failure and disaster as His people trust in Him. In their being deceived by the Gibeonites, Israel was reaping what it had sown. Ironically, just as the sons of Israel "spoke deceitfully" to the Hivites while the patriarch Jacob was still alive (see Gen.

34:13), so now the children of Israel in turn find themselves deceived by the Hivites.

But Israel, even though they failed to seek counsel from God and let the ambassadors from Gibeon dupe them, nonetheless gained loyal allies in Canaan. Once the Gibeonites made the covenant with Israel, they stayed true to their word, pulled out of the Canaanite confederacy, broke blood ties with the other Hivites who later fought against Israel, and remained loyal in the midst of God's people.

The Gibeonites themselves also learned that apparent disaster and even a curse can be turned into a blessing. Once citizens of "a great city, like one of the royal cities," in which "all its men were mighty" (Joshua 10:2), the Gibeonites "had adopted the garb of poverty for the purpose of deception, and it was fastened upon them as a badge of perpetual servitude" (*Patriarchs and Prophets*, p. 507). They were to be "woodcutters and water carriers" for Israel (Joshua 9:21, 23, 27). Thus was literally fulfilled the curse of Noah upon Canaan (Gen. 9:25, 26; 10:17).

Although such humiliating punishment may seem at first glance almost worse than death itself, it turned out to be a great blessing for the Gibeonites. For even though they became hewers of wood and drawers of water, their service would be done, according to Joshua, "for the house of my God" (verse 23), "for the altar of the Lord, in the place which He would choose" (verse 27). The curse gave them a special place of blessing near the presence of God! The later history of Gibeon reveals the high religious privileges eventually afforded to this city and demonstrates their loyalty in remaining among God's people (see Joshua 21:17; 1 Kings 3:3-15; 1 Chron. 12:4; 16:39; 21:29; 2 Chron. 1:1-13; Neh. 3:7; 7:25). Thus the curse turned into a blessing!

"From my perch atop the Muslim mosque on Mount Nebî Samwîl, I now look not to Jerusalem to the south and east, nor to the Mediterranean Sea to the west, nor to Old Testament Gibeon to the north. Instead, holding my hat from blowing off in the brisk late afternoon breeze, I look directly below me to the archaeological excavations currently in progress all around the Muslim mosque and its adjoining Jewish shrine on the summit of the mountain.

"In the time of Solomon this mountain was known as the great high place of Gibeon. Here the sanctuary was located during the reign of David and Solomon, before the Temple in Jerusalem was built (1 Chron. 16:39, 40; 21:29; 2 Chron. 1:3, 6, 13). Here Solomon sacrificed and prayed for wisdom in his dream (1 Kings 3:4-15). And here on this very spot the tabernacle stood for many years, and the converted Gibeonites from the nearby city and its three satellite towns (see Joshua 9:17) brought wood and water for the needs of the sanctuary.

"The current excavations may uncover some evidence for the tabernacle that stood on this site during the time of David and Solomon—and may even uncover some of the holy water pots of the Gibeonites as they performed their service to the Lord. But if no such artifacts or other material evidence emerges, there already exists a witness to the Gibeonites that will never be lost—the biblical record of a curse turned into a great blessing."

Do you have setbacks in your life, like Israel, caused by the subterfuge of Satan? Do you suffer from "curses," like the Gibeonites, resulting from your dishonesty or other moral failures? By the grace of God, He can transform each setback into victory, each curse into a blessing! Only let Him! Ask Him right now.

----

[1] For the more complete popular description of the excavations at Gibeon by the excavator, see J. B. Pritchard, *Gibeon, Where the Sun Stood Still: The Discovery of the Biblical City* (Princeton, N.J.: Princeton University Press, 1962).

[2] Katherine Kersten, "How the Feminist Establishment Hurts Women: A Christian Critique of a Movement Gone Wrong," *Christianity Today,* June 20, 1994, p. 24.

Canaan's Conquest Completed

9

Francis Schaeffer perceptively analyzes major battle strategies in World War II and compares them with Joshua's divinely inspired tactics for the conquest of Canaan:

"We can think of three campaigns in World War II in which geography affected tactics. When the Germans entered France, their tactic was to drive a wedge into the middle of France and then expand in both directions. When the Greeks were fighting the Italians, the Italians took the plain and the Greeks took the hills. As a result, the Greeks controlled the situation even with less-well-armed forces. The English smashed strongholds first and then fanned out into weaker areas. If we combine these three tactics of warfare, we have a picture of the God-given strategy for Joshua's campaign to take the land."[1]

Schaeffer continues[2] to describe how Joshua drove a wedge through the center of the country of Palestine by conquering Jericho and then marching through the wadis (dry riverbeds) from Gilgal up into the central hill country to take Ai and later Gibeon. From their vantage point in control of the hill country, Israel swiftly expanded their wedge to the south (the southern campaign, Joshua 10) and to the north (the northern campaign, Joshua 11). They first conquered the strongholds, and then later undertook the mop-up operations against the resistance that remained.

In short, God provided Joshua with a brilliant campaign strategy, and under divine blessing, Israel's commander executed it marvelously.

During my recent stay in Israel I had the privilege of retracing the footsteps of Joshua and his army as they conducted their military conquests and "the Lord fought for Israel" (Joshua 10:14, 42; cf. 11:8). Come, let us together plunge into the battle and taste the victory!

The Southern Campaign

I invite you to consult a map of Joshua's campaigns as we follow the movements of his troops. We go first to the five cities south of Gibeon, whose kings entered into a coalition against Gibeon after it had joined forces with Israel. The leader of the Amorite confederation was Adoni-Zedek, king of Jerusalem, who invited the kings of four other cities to participate in the attack.

Hebron (also called Kiriath Arba, Joshua 20:7), about 20 miles south of Jerusalem and the highest city in the central mountains of Palestine (3,300 ft), was the former home of Abraham; burial place of Abraham, Isaac, Jacob, Rebekah, and Leah; and at the time of the conquest, home of the giant sons of Anak. Jarmuth (modern Khirbet Yarmûk), some 16 miles southwest of Jerusalem in the Shephelah, occupied a commanding position between the Valley of Elah (where David later fought Goliath) and the Valley of Sorek (famous for the exploits of Samson), with a view into the coastal plain. Lachish (modern Tell ed-Duweir), about 25 miles southwest of Jerusalem and farther down in the Shephelah, guarded the main road from Egypt to Palestine and later became one of Judah's most important frontier fortresses on the south. Eglon (probably modern Tell el-Hesī), some seven miles west of Lachish, occupies the edge of the Shephelah or foothills.

After one visits these sites, it becomes apparent that the biblical account is geographically precise. We read that Adoni-Zedek called for the other kings to "come up" to the north and (except for Hebron) to ascend in elevation to Jerusalem, to join in the confederacy (Joshua 10:4).

Soon the Amorite armies camped in the valley surrounding Gibeon. The besieged city sent word to Joshua in Gilgal, pleading: "Do not forsake your servants; come up to us quickly, save us and help us" (verse 6). This time Joshua did not fail to seek counsel from the Lord and received the divine assurance that He would deliver the enemy into the hands of Israel's army. So Joshua and his forces marched all night up from Gilgal, probably through the Wadi Qilt, a distance of about 25 miles and a climb in elevation of 3,300 feet.

My son Jonathan and I wanted to experience some of the rugged terrain and rigorous travel of the hosts of Israel that night, and so we backpacked through the Wadi Qilt about the same time of year that Joshua and his army would have made the trip. However, we took the easier way, hiking *down* through the wadi, instead of up, and not starting at the very beginning of the wadi.

Nonetheless, we found the route no gentle stroll! It was necessary to scramble over a seemingly never-ending number of gigantic boulders and ford the stream (or walk through the streambed) numerous times. Much of the way the wadi was actually a gorge with walls rising precipitously several hundred feet on either side. We spent the night in the middle of the gorge, camped on a rock ledge looking out over the streambed. A full day we hiked, and after a night's rest we continued several hours the next day before seeing the plain of the Jordan and the vicinity of Jericho and ancient Gilgal open up before us. We gained a new appreciation for the stamina of Joshua's men, who in the moonlight had pushed forward 25 miles through the wilderness of Judah, ascending more than 3,000 feet in elevation on the rugged route, and yet at the break of day were ready to *begin* the battle!

"I look out over the valley surrounding Gibeon from Mount Nebî-Samwîl, the highest point in the vicinity. I see before my imagination the sprawling camp of the Amorite confederacy under the command of King Adoni-Zedek, just waking up when Joshua and his men initiate their surprise frontal attack. I watch the entire Amorite army 'rushing about madly,' 'thrown into panic and confusion' (this is the force of the Hebrew word *hāmam* in verse 10). A great slaughter takes place at Gibeon, and in my mind's eye the fleeing Amorites head northwest along the road to Upper Beth Horon. There they race headlong down the steep and rugged path that descends more than 700 feet through the narrow pass to Lower Beth Horon . . .

"Now I drive to the lookout over the 'descent of Beth Horon' (verse 11) and see the twisting and winding modern road dropping through the narrow defile to the Valley of Aijalon below. Here in my imagination I relive the mighty miracle that happened in this pass. I see the large hailstones that the Lord cast from heaven upon the fleeing forces of the Amorites. I see Joshua standing near my position on the ridge at the top of the pass, looking up to the noon-day sun hovering over Gibeon behind him to the east and then to the waning moon faintly visible over the Valley of Aijalon in front of him to the west. He realizes that he needs more than one after-noon to overtake the enemy and completely rout them before they can return to their fortified cities to the southwest. And inspired by the Spirit of God, he prays for what never happened before or since in the history of the world:

> " ' "Sun, stand still over Gibeon;
>   And Moon, in the Valley of Aijalon."
> So the sun stood still,
> And the moon stopped,
> Till the people had revenge
> Upon their enemies' (verses 12, 13).

"The sun and moon remained in their same position in the sky for another whole day. Mind-boggling! It is indeed true: 'There has been no day like that, before it or after it, that the Lord heeded the voice of a man; for the Lord fought for Israel' (verse 14).

"At this site, as the ancient battle and miracle of the longest day faded from my imagination, I found myself remembering the secret of Joshua's victory: 'The man who commanded, "Sun, stand thou still upon Gibeon; and thou, Moon, in the valley of Ajalon," is the man who for hours lay prostrate upon the earth in prayer in the camp at Gilgal. The men of prayer are the men of power' *(Patriarchs and Prophets, p. 509).*

"I find myself praying to the same God as Joshua: 'Lord, if You have that much power to route the Amorites with mighty hailstones from Your heavenly arsenal, and to make the sun and moon stand still, however You did it,[3] then I know You are able to care for my every need, to deliver me from every trouble, to give me victory over my spiritual enemies. I choose again to be a man of prevailing prayer. And I invite You to fight for me as You did for Israel of old.

Thank You for being such an all-powerful, all-loving God! Amen.'"

During our travels this spring, we also retraced the path of the Israelite army in routing its enemies as they fled through the Valley of Aijalon and to the southwest. We traversed the region of Makkedah (the exact site has not yet been positively identified), observing the numerous caves in the area, in one of which were hidden, and later buried, the five kings of the enemy confederation. Also, we visited or drove by the various cities that Joshua conquered in his southern campaign: Makkedah, Libnah (probably modern Tell es-Sâfî, 21 miles west of Bethlehem), Gezer (modern Tell Gezer, 18 miles northwest of Jerusalem), Lachish, Eglon, Hebron, and Debir (probably Khirbet Rabud, 7½ miles southwest of Hebron).

The Northern Campaign

We traversed the northern region of modern Israel, and at Tell Hazor, in the Huleh plain, some 10 miles north of the Sea of Galilee, I imagined Jabin the king summoning all the kings of the northern region.

"Wednesday, April 27. I look out from Tell Hazor over the nearby fertile and well-irrigated valley, the ancient waters of Merom, and visualize an army camped there with 'as many people as the sand that is on the seashore in multitude, with very many horses and chariots' (Joshua 11:4). I imagine this great multitude arrayed against Joshua. But God has assured him of a total victory before the next day was over. I see Joshua and his men of war suddenly attacking the countless hosts of the enemy and picture how 'the Lord delivered them into the hand of Israel, who . . . attacked them until they left none of them remaining' (verse 8). Then I picture Joshua turning back and taking the great fortified capital of the north, Hazor, destroying its inhabitants and burning the city. The smoke rises from the tell, with snow-capped Mount Hermon in the distance, like a silent witness. What a great victory was this!"

Why the Divine Command to Destroy the Canaanites?

Before concluding our discussion of the conquest in the book of Joshua, it may be well to consider some questions concerning God's character that may have arisen in your mind as you read about the bloody slaughter of the inhabitants of Canaan. Why did God command Israel to destroy the Canaanites at the time of the conquest? Was God justified in calling for what amounted to genocide—the destruction of a whole nation, in fact, a group of nations, including women and children? Or was it not really God's will that they be destroyed but because Israel would have considered anything else unjust, God condescended to their warped sense of justice?

If such slaughter was justifiable, why was Israel asked to do the slaughtering? Would not such wholesale bloodshed lessen the value of human life as they witnessed and participated in repeated scenes of violence?

Such questions boil down to two major issues. The first concerns theodicy—the justification of God's actions. We must place our question in the larger context of God's attitude toward people who had totally given themselves over to evil—individuals, cities, nations, and the whole world—prior to the time of Israel's entrance into Canaan. For the antediluvian world; for Sodom and Gomorrah; for Korah, Dathan, and Abiram; for the Amalekites—God consistently gave a time of probation that, when unheeded, was followed by an investigative and executive judgment (Gen. 6:1-13; 18, 19; Ex. 17; Num. 16).

More than 400 years before Israel's conquest of Canaan, God announced that Abraham could not yet possess the Promised Land because "the iniquity of the Amorites is not yet complete" (Gen. 15:16). The Lord gave time for the inhabitants of Canaan to repent, and we have evidence that He had his servants working to reach the people of Canaan during that era (see Gen. 14:17-20; Num. 22-24). Further evidence came to the inhabitants of Canaan as they heard about God's mighty acts in delivering His people during the Exodus and in the wilderness wanderings (see Joshua 2:9-11).

At the time of the conquest the iniquity of the Amorites was indeed full. "The Canaanites had abandoned themselves to the foulest and most debasing heathenism. . . . Like the men before the Flood, the Canaanites lived only to blaspheme Heaven and defile the earth. And both love and justice demanded the prompt execution of these rebels against God and foes to man" (*Patriarchs and Prophets*, p. 492).

The Ras Shamra (Ugaritic) tablets dating from about the time of Joshua reveal details of gross sexual orgies—too vile to print here—practiced among the Canaanites as the very high point of their fertility cult religious rituals.[4] Religious belief encouraged worshipers to engage in ritual intercourse with the cult prostitutes at the high places in order to emulate and stimulate the sex activities of the fertility gods and thereby bring fertility to the land. Figurines and plaques of nude female figures with exaggerated sexual features, often connected with a phallic symbol, have turned up at almost every major excavation of Canaanite sites in Palestine.[5] Archaeologist William F. Albright describes the sensuous and carnal character of the Canaanite goddesses, concluding that the erotic aspect of Canaanite worship "must have sunk to extremely sordid depths of social degradation."[6]

Ancient texts also give accounts of child sacrifice.[7] Further accounts reveal the insatiable thirst for blood and ghastly love of violence that characterized the Canaanite gods and goddesses. For example, one describes the Canaanite goddess Anath—patroness of sex and war—as carrying out a general massacre followed by an unbelievably gory scene:

"The blood was so deep that she waded in it up to her knees—nay, up to her neck. Under her feet were human heads, above her human hands flew like locusts. In her sensuous delight she decorated herself with suspended heads while she attached hands to her girdle. Her joy at the butchery is described in even more sadistic language: 'Her liver swelled with laughter, her heart was full of joy, the liver of Anath (was full of) exultation (?).' Afterwards Anath 'was satisfied' and washed her hands in human gore before proceeding to other occupations."[8]

A people can rise no higher than the concept of god and religion that they possess. With such conceptions and practices of sex and violence at the core of Canaanite religion, it is not surprising that within a few centuries (the 400 years of divine probation) a whole civilization had lost its moral capacity to respond to the promptings of God's Spirit. God in His mercy, as much as His justice, declared that nothing remained but to bring their existence to an end.

The second issue concerns why God commanded Israel to carry out the execution. Does not the sixth commandment forbid killing? Again, a closer look at the larger context reveals that God's injunction did not violate the sixth commandment. The Hebrew word for "kill" is the more restricted Hebrew term that refers primarily to murder and manslaughter, and does not include capital punishment or divinely commanded warfare.

Furthermore, we must recognize that it was apparently not God's original plan that Israel would need to destroy the Canaanites (at least primarily) by their own hands. Ellen White insightfully notes in discussing the incident of rebellion at Kadesh Barnea: "The Lord had never commanded them [Israel] to 'go up and fight.' It was not His purpose that they should gain the land by warfare, but by strict obedience to His commands" (Patriarchs and Prophets, p. 392). God had promised to send His Angel and natural forces (hornets) before them to take care of the enemy inhabitants (Ex. 23:23, 28). At the beginning of Israel's history at the Exodus, and later when they had sufficient faith, God fought the battles for them while they stood still and witnessed His acts of salvation (see Ex. 14, 15; 2 Kings 19; 2 Chron. 32; Isa. 37). Throughout the conquest, God often used supernatural means (divinely inspired confusion, earthquake, hailstones, etc.) and discomfited the enemy before Joshua and his army.

As a result of Israel's lack of faith, God did condescend to meet them where they were and allowed them to fight, promising to go with them and give them victory. But His condescension did not compromise the standard of His law or distort truth.

Thus God's character stands vindicated in His just and merciful command for the conquest of Canaan and the destruction of its inhabitants. The conquest shows God's willingness to work with His people at whatever level He finds them, but also reveals His continual call to a higher level of trust in divine power.

Summary of Conquest: Type and Antitype

This spring I visited most of the 31 cities mentioned in Joshua 12 in the approximate order that Joshua conquered them during the some seven years of the conquest (see Joshua 11:17, 18; 14:6-10). I wrote in my journal on such sites as Jericho, Jerusalem, Hebron, Lachish, Gezer, Arad, Aphek, Hazor, Megiddo, and Dor, and scribbled notes as we visited or drove by many others. Now back in the U.S.A., I look over my journal entries and view the slides of the terrain at the battle sites and the desolate tells or mounds marking the cities Joshua defeated.

The full force of the conquest begins to dawn upon my consciousness. By implicitly following God's battle strategy, combining their trust in divine power with earnest human effort, Joshua and the armies of Israel gloriously succeeded in the conquest of Canaan. Joshua "left nothing undone [literally, turned aside from nothing] of all that the Lord had commanded Moses. So Joshua took all this land: the mountain country, all the South [the Negeb], all the land of Goshen, the lowland [the Shephelah] and the Jordan plain [the Arabah]. . . . Then the land rested from war" (Joshua 11:15-23).

The typological implication is profound and powerful! Jesus the new Joshua also conquered His enemies by trusting completely in the Father's battle plan for His life. And the new Joshua wants to give His people, spiritual Israel, that same kind of glorious success in their spiritual warfare against sin and Satan. Shall we claim that abundant victory?

We also can look forward to the end of the great controversy, at the battle of Armageddon, when Satan's forces are poised to destroy God's people. At that time the Lord will bring out of His armory hailstones as "weapons of His indignation" (Jer. 50:25; see Job 38:22, 23; Rev. 16:17, 21). Again, after the millennium, as in the earthly Promised Land, the camp of God faces the enemy's final frontal attack. At last the conquest will be consummated. As with the five kings, all enemies will be put under the feet of our Conqueror (Joshua 10:24, 25; Ps. 110:1). And as with Jericho, Ai, and Hazor, the fire will do its destroying and cleansing work (see Rev. 20).

As I work on this chapter, my son Jonathan walks excitedly into my study with the words, "Dad, summer has just begun, at 9:48 a.m.! It's the longest day of the year." He's right—the longest daylight of the year here in Michigan, a few hours longer than the shortest daylight period. But I remind myself, this "longest day" is nothing compared to Joshua's longest day!

And then I think again. Joshua's longest day is nothing compared to the longest day of the new Joshua. During the final battle and afterward, when God makes the earth new, in the holy city of the New Jerusalem, there is *no night!* There the longest day will last an eternity. The Sun of righteousness, rising with healing in His wings, will never set. For eternity "the Lamb is its light" (Rev. 21:23).

Please join me now in making an appointment with our new Joshua to be there with Him for the eternal day!

---

[1] Francis A. Schaeffer, *Joshua and the Flow of Biblical History* (London: Hodder and Stoughton, 1975), p. 93.

[2] *Ibid.*

[3] The miracle of the sun standing still is so incredible to modern scientific thinking that commentators have sought to give various poetic hyperbolic explanations for the meaning of the text, such as an eclipse, cloud cover, or prolonged morning mist. But the Hebrew is clear and unambiguous (Joshua 10:13) that the sun stood still in its course across the sky. The word for "stood still" in verses 12 and 13 is ʿāmad ("stand, stand still, stop), the same word used in Joshua 3:16 to indicate that the waters of the Jordan River "stood still" or stopped flowing. I do not pretend to know the geophysical mechanism God used to perform the miracle of the longest day, but God is certainly more powerful than the "natural laws" He has created, and He can suspend or alter such laws at will, should He so choose. In this case the miracle not only gave Joshua more time to defeat his enemies, but served as a demonstration of the powerlessness of the Canaanite deities—the storm god Baal and the sun god Shamash, as well as the moon deity—in contrast to the one true God, Yahweh, the omnipotent One.

[4] See John Gray, *Legacy of Canaan, Vetus Testamentum* Supplements, vol. 5, revised ed. (Leiden: Brill, 1965), pp. 98-103, for translations of archaeological texts from Ras Shamra, giving explicit and revolting details of the ritual accompanying sexual orgies on the high places.

[5] For sample pictures and descriptions, see J. B. Pritchard, ed., *The Ancient Near East in Pictures* (Princeton, N.J.: University of Princeton Press, 1969), pp. 160-165, 197, 198, 470-473.

[6] William F. Albright, *Archaeology and the Religion of Israel* (Baltimore: Johns Hopkins Press, 1942, 1968), p. 77.

[7] See A.R.W. Green, *The Role of Human Sacrifice in the Ancient Near East* (Missoula, Mont.: Scholars Press, 1975); cf. Lev. 18:21; 2 Kings 17:17; 21:6; 23:10; 2 Chron. 28:1, 3; 33:1, 6; Jer. 7:31; 19:4, 5; 32:35; Eze. 16:21; 23:37, 39.

[8] Albright, p. 77.

Divide
the Land!

10

I write these lines on June 6, my birthday. It is also the fiftieth an-niversary of D-day in World War II. The newspapers, maga-zines, TV, and radio have been highlighting that day in 1944 that changed the course of history. Ceremonies are taking place at Omaha Beach as I write, with the chief dignitaries of major coun-tries of the world participating. Though D-day did not mean the immediate end to the war, nevertheless, the struggle on the shores of France that occurred that day constituted the decisive battle that broke the back of the enemy and assured the freedom and total victory that came at V-E Day.

The illustrations of D-day and V-E Day in World War II provide a rough modern parallel that helps us to understand the apparent con-tradiction that we find in the two halves of the book of Joshua.

As we complete the first half of the book, in the summary of the conquest in Joshua 11 and 12, we could easily get the impres-sion that the entire war of conquest is over and Israel has already realized total victory. We read that "Joshua took the whole land, according to all that the Lord had said to Moses; and Joshua gave it as an inheritance to Israel according to their divisions by their tribes. Then the land rested from war" (Joshua 11:23). But when we come to the second half of the book, starting in Joshua 13, it appears that Israel still had much conquering yet to do. We hear God say to Joshua, "There remains very much land yet to be pos-sessed" (Joshua 13:1). Scripture tells of tribe after tribe that failed to flush out the inhabitants of major segments of their inheritance

(Joshua 13:13; 15:63; 16:10; 17:12, 13). And Joshua declares to seven of the tribes, "How long will you neglect to go and possess the land which the Lord God of your fathers has given you?" (Joshua 18:3).

The Already and the Not Yet

The answer to this apparent contradiction is the difference between D-day and V-E Day. Joshua 11:16 and 23 indicate that Joshua "took" [Hebrew, *lāqaḥ]* the land. The Hebrew word *lāqaḥ* implies that he had broken the back of the resistance and taken control of the region, even though Israelite forces had not conquered and occupied every city. As a result of Joshua's "taking" the land, "the land rested [Hebrew, *šāqat]* from war" (verse 23). The Hebrew word *šāqat* simply means "to be quiet." The land was quiet because the decisive battles were over and the back of the enemy resistance had been broken. Israel's "D-day" had occurred.

When we come to the end of Joshua's life, however, we read that "the Lord God gave them rest [Hebrew, *nûaḥ]* all around" (Joshua 21:44). The Hebrew word *nûaḥ* means "to rest, settle down, and remain in repose." Israel now had "settled rest and repose" because "the Lord had delivered all their enemies into their hands" (verse 44). It was this kind of *nûaḥ* rest, and not just *šāqat* quietness, that God had promised Israel before the conquest began (see Deut. 3:20; 12:10; 25:19; Joshua 1:13, 15). Israel's "V-E Day" had arrived.

Ellen White clearly portrays the situation at the end of the major campaigns of Joshua, before the division of the inheritance: "But though the power of the Canaanites had been broken, they had not been fully dispossessed" *(Patriarchs and Prophets*, p. 511).

The paradox between the "taking" of the land and the full "possessing of the possessions" has parallels in the Christian life. A tension exists between the already and the not yet, or in technical terms, between inaugurated and consummated eschatology.[1] Many biblical passages affirm this. For example, Paul speaks of receiving the "Spirit of adoption" in one breath (Rom. 8:15), but in the next he indicates that we are still "waiting for the adoption, the redemption of our body" (verse 23). The Epistle of Hebrews utilizes the typology of Joshua in the same way: believers have already entered into spiritual rest (Heb. 4:3, 10), and yet the book admonishes them to "be diligent to enter that rest" (verse 11).

The witness of the New Testament is consistent throughout. The victory worked out by Jesus in His life and death and resurrection has broken the back of the enemy. Satan has been cast down, the D-day battle has been fought, and our inheritance of the land has been assured. But we still must "possess our possessions." And the final V-E Day still lies ahead. We are living between the "already" (Jesus "taking" the land) and the "not yet" (the complete "dispossessing" of the enemy).

Apportioning the Land—Joshua and Jesus

As we have already noted in chapter 2, Joshua is a type of the Messiah in His work of dividing Israel's inheritance. In Isa. 49:8 the Father foretells one of the missions of His Servant, the Messiah: "I will preserve You and give You as a covenant to the people, to restore the earth, *to cause them to inherit the desolate heritages [margin, inheritances]*." It is the same language used to describe the work of Joshua (Deut. 1:38; 3:28; 31:7; Joshua 1:6). Just as Joshua divided the inheritance to literal Israel, so Jesus, the antitypical Joshua, receives and appoints an inheritance for His saints (Heb. 1:4; 9:15). Believers receive their spiritual inheritance already in this life (Acts 20:32; Eph. 1:11, 14, 18) and will receive their final inheritance in the new earth (Matt. 25:34; Col. 3:24; Rev. 21:7).

"Give Me This Mountain!"

Before Joshua begins to apportion Israel's inheritance, Caleb, now the oldest man in Israel except for Joshua, arrives with the elders of his tribe of Judah. He reminds Joshua of the promise made to him by the Lord, through Moses, when as a faithful spy he had "wholly followed the Lord" (Joshua 14:9; cf. Num. 14:24; Deut. 1:34, 36).

His character had not changed since he spied out the land 45 years before: "Caleb's faith now was just what it was when his testimony had contradicted the evil report of the spies. He had believed God's promise that He would put His people in possession of Canaan, and in this he had followed the Lord fully. . . . He did not ask for himself a land already conquered, but the place which above all others the spies had thought it impossible to subdue. By the help of God he would wrest this stronghold from the very giants whose power had staggered the faith of Israel. It was no desire for honor or aggrandizement that prompted Caleb's request. The brave old warrior was desirous of giving to the people an example that would honor God, and encourage the tribes fully to subdue the land which their fathers had deemed unconquerable" *(Patriarchs and Prophets*, pp. 512, 513).

One of my favorite passages in the Bible is Caleb's request, "Give me this mountain" (Joshua 14:12). Perhaps I am somewhat prejudiced because of my love of mountains. But the spiritual impact of his fearless request is awesome. We have many spiritual "mountains" that loom ahead of us in possessing our spiritual inheritance. May God give us the courage and faith to say, like Caleb, "Give me this mountain!"

He gave a shining example to others in Israel by following through in "possessing his possessions." After the conquest of the giant stronghold of Hebron, he "pushed on to further conquests for the benefit of the nation and the glory of God" *(Patriarchs and Prophets*, p. 513).

His experience reminds me of the last stanzas of one of my favorite poems:

> "In the world's broad field of battle,
>   In the bivouac of life,
> Be not like dumb, driven cattle!
>   Be a hero in the strife!

> "Trust no Future, howe'er pleasant!
>   Let the dead Past bury its dead!
> Act,—act in the living Present!
>   Heart within, and God o'erhead!

> "Lives of great men all remind us
>   We can make our lives sublime,
> And, departing, leave behind us
>   Footprints on the sands of time—

> "Footprints, that perhaps another,

Sailing o'er life's solemn main,
A forlorn and shipwrecked brother,
Seeing, shall take heart again.

"Let us, then, be up and doing,
With a heart for any fate;
Still achieving, still pursuing,
Learn to labor and to wait."[2]

Levi, Judah, and Joseph

The time now came for the apportionment of the inheritance to the nine and a half tribes on the west side of the Jordan River. The tribe of Levi did not receive land because their inheritance was "the sacrifices of the Lord God of Israel made by fire" (Joshua 13:14), "the Lord God of Israel" (verse 33), and "the priesthood of the Lord" (Joshua 18:7).

The first tribes to receive their inheritance were Judah and Joseph. Why did they get their inheritance before lots were cast for the other seven tribes? Already in his predictive blessing of the 12 sons/tribes, Jacob singles out Judah and Joseph for special blessings and couches them in Messianic terms.[3] These two tribes predominate in Israel's later history, and in the divided monarchy give their names to the northern and southern kingdoms (Ephraim and Judah, respectively). Apparently with a view toward God's special plan for Judah and Ephraim, already predicted in the Torah, Joshua, that faithful meditator upon the books of Moses, sets these tribes apart in the apportioning process. They are to receive the heart of the land of Canaan.

The Inner Chamber of Jewels

I invite you to consult a map of Palestine for the time of Joshua (see for example, *SDA Bible Dictionary*, Map VI) as you read Joshua 13:1-17:13. Trace the boundaries and major cities of the inheritance given to the two and a half tribes east of the Jordan by Moses, and to the tribes of Judah and Joseph west of the Jordan. While you're at it, you might also do the same for the focus of our next chapter: the other seven tribes recorded in Joshua 18, 19, and the six cities of refuge and 48 Levitical cities listed in Joshua 20, 21.

It has been rightly said that "if the Bible is a geographical storehouse, then this book [Joshua] is its inner chamber of jewels."[4] I have found it fascinating to try to locate the various cities and boundaries of each of the 12 tribes of Israel. Some of the "jewels" are hidden treasure, since their exact location remains unknown. Like a long-lost treasure map, many of the landmarks so familiar then—a tree here (for example, Joshua 24:26), a stone there (for example, Joshua 15:6), small towns and villages, springs and wells—are either difficult to identify or no longer traceable. But patient research tracking the clues of the biblical treasure map has led to the modern discovery of many of these "lost jewels."

It is also highly illuminating to read Bible dictionary discussions of some of the major sites from the time of Joshua, such as Heshbon, Beersheba, Lachish, Ekron, Ashdod, En-gedi, Beth Shean, Dor, Taanach, and Megiddo. Pictorial Bible dictionaries and atlases have photographs of many of these sites. For me personally to read about, see photos of, and even visit such sites has been a wonderful experience! The Bible has come to life as I have been able to picture its background geography. No wonder Ellen White calls such information "practical knowledge." "An understanding of the customs of those who lived in Bible times, of the *location* and time of events, is *practical knowledge;* for it aids in making clear the figures of the Bible and in bringing out the force of Christ's lessons" (*Counsels to Parents and Teachers*, p. 518; italics supplied).

Women's Rights!

The inheritance for Manesseh (one of the sons of Joseph) includes provision for the daughters of Zelophehad (Joshua 17:3, 4; cf. Num. 26:33, 34; 27:1-5). It gives a divine perspective on the value of womanhood. "This incident showed a larger regard for the rights of women than is usually conceded for that time. It established the principle that a woman was not a mere chattel, with no rights of her own. Wherever the principles of the true God have been established, there the state of womanhood has been exalted" (*The SDA Bible Commentary,* vol. 2, p. 261).

We might well consider whether our own attitudes and the climate of our local churches exalt the state and value of womanhood, and give modern "daughters of Zelophehad" their rightful spiritual inheritance.

Stopping Halfway

In contrast to Caleb and the daughters of Zelophehad, who had legitimate rights and displayed a noble spirit, representatives of the tribe of Joseph approach Joshua after receiving their inheritance with a different spirit (see Joshua 17:14-18). They request more land since their tribe is "a great [numerous] people" (verse 14), but the real cause for their complaint is a lack of faith and courage to drive out the Canaanites, Perizzites, and the giants that dwell in their allotted territory. Joshua deftly turns their arguments on their heads by replying in effect, "If you are so great and numerous as you say, then you should be well able to drive out the inhabitants of your inheritance!" He points out that their inheritance was really more than one allotment already, because they had the vast forests of the hill country of central Palestine, which were thinly populated. If they would only assert themselves, they could clear the forests and enlarge their territory. By occupying the mountain country, they would also command its "outgoings"—its wadis leading into the valleys. With this advantage and the blessing of the Lord, Joshua assures them, "You shall drive out the Canaanites, though they have iron chariots and are strong" (verse 18).

Joshua's encouragement for the tribe of Joseph to dispossess the Canaanites in their territory reflected God's plan for all of the tribes. Unfortunately, a refrain runs throughout Joshua 13-18, a refrain of "stopping halfway" in possessing their inheritance. The tribes east of the Jordan stopped halfway and failed to fully dispossess the Geshurites and the Maachathites (Joshua 13:13). The tribe of Judah could not drive out the Jebusites that inhabited Jerusalem (Joshua 15:63). The tribe of Ephraim did not remove the Canaanites in Gezer (Joshua 16:10). The tribe of Manasseh did not push out the Canaanites from a number of the strategic cities that were part of their allotted inheritance: Beth Shean, Ibleam, Dor, En Dor, Taanach, and Megiddo (Joshua 17:11-13).

The same litany of "stopping halfway" occurs in later chapters of Joshua and also in the book of Judges. The tribe of Dan seems to have allowed the portion of their inheritance in the level valleys to slip away from them as they found themselves forced into the mountains by their powerful Amorite neighbors (see Judges 1:34). Apparently they went north and occupied a territory of their own choosing at Dan (Joshua 19:47).[5] The book of Judges mentions other tribes with the same failure: Benjamin, Zebulun, Asher, and Naphtali (Judges 1:21, 30-36).

As I visited most of these territories and individual sites these past few weeks, I could empathize with the children of Israel. One cannot help being impressed with the massive fortifications of these ancient Canaanite strongholds. And one can understand how the seemingly impregnable walls, the chariots, and the mighty (and often gigantic) warriors would give pause for caution, temptation to delay, inertia, and negligence.

Cowardice and lack of faith led to compromise. As Israel became a stronger nation, it conscripted many of these cities into forced labor, but never completely dispossessed the inhabitants as God had commanded. The leavening influence of such people was clearly one of the principal contributing factors that led to Israel's downward slide into idolatry and eventual apostasy (see Judges 2, 3).

And cowardice and faltering faith still lead to compromise today. Will we hear the warning sounded by failures of ancient Israel and urgently press forward with faith to completely dispossess the "Canaanites" in our lives? We need not repeat the same slide into apostasy—God is alive and ready to give us victory over the "iron chariots" and "giants" that would overpower us! Come, let us completely "possess our possessions" in Christ!

"Wednesday, April 27, early morning. I write these lines on the summit of Tell Beth Shean—one of the cities Israel failed to conquer and dispossess its inhabitants. I read in my guidebook of the 18 layers of successive cities on this massive tell, some 250 feet high. Seeing the excavations of the Canaanite temple to Ashtarte, I recoiled, imagining the debased fertility cult rituals that took place there. Beth Shean was a formidable city—and also a silent witness to Israel's lack of faith and failure to follow through on possessing their possessions.

"Above the mound in the distance to the southwest are the hills of Gilboa, where the Philistines killed Saul and Jonathan—a witness to the fruit of compromise centuries before. Oh, how God longed to completely drive out the Canaanites and the Philistines, but Israel's faith was not strong enough to take hold of the promises of God and complete the conquest. . . .

" 'Lord, here on the summit of Tell Beth Shean this morning, I pray for You to increase my faith. I choose anew to allow You to drive out the giants and conquer the walled cities in my spiritual experience. You are faithful and trustworthy—I dedicate myself to cooperating with the heavenly agencies and winning through against the enemy! Thank You for hearing in the name of the heavenly Joshua! Amen.' "

---

[1] See our brief discussion of this in chapter 2. For more detailed biblical evidence, see especially George Eldon Ladd, *The Presence of the Future: The Eschatology of Biblical Realism* (Grand Rapids: Eerdmans, 1974).

[2] From Henry Wadsworth Longfellow (1807-1882), "A Psalm of Life."

[3] In Genesis 49:10 Jacob predicts of Judah: "The scepter shall not depart from Judah, nor a lawgiver from between his feet, until Shiloh ["Peace giver," the Messiah] comes; and to Him shall be the obedience of the people." In verses 22-27 he describes the future of the tribe of Joseph in Messianic terms, highlighting the suffering of the antitypical Joseph (verse 23), and that He will be "the Shepherd, the Stone of Israel" (verse 24). These two prophecies—one of the Messiah's royal mission, and one of His path of suffering—merge in Jesus, the antitypical fulfillment of both.

[4] Frederick J. Bliss, *The Development of Palestinian Exploration* (New York: Charles Scribner's Son, 1906), p. 11.

[5] See *The SDA Bible Commentary,* vol. 2, pp. 275, 276 for a discussion of this situation.

Dividing the Inheritance—Stage II

11

Sunday, April 24. As I write these lines, I sit on Tell Shiloh, the site of ancient Shiloh, where Israel set up the tabernacle of God after the conquest of Canaan. I have just stepped off the dimensions of the ancient sanctuary enclosure—some 75 feet by 150 feet—on the artificially created terrace at the northern end of the tell, and find that the sanctuary precincts would have fit precisely on this flat, hewn-rock terrace.

"I sit on a slightly raised rock cutting that very possibly served as the Most Holy Place for the ancient Israelite sanctuary. Again and again I tell myself to let the significance of this site sink in: Joshua brought the tabernacle probably to this very spot! I recall that for 300 years this was the place where the Shekinah glory hovered over the ark of the covenant, and where all Israel came to worship at the annual festivals. I imagine where the courtyard, holy place, and Most Holy Place probably once stood, visualizing the various articles of furniture in place and mentally reenacting the daily services that took place here.

"In my mind's eye I see Joshua the son of Nun and the high priest, Eleazar, standing at the door of the tabernacle of meeting, dividing the inheritance of Israel by lot (see Joshua 18:10). I find myself sending up a brief prayer, 'Thank You, Lord, for the sanctuary and its services, and all that they teach us about the gospel and Your present work in the heavenly sanctuary, the great original after which this earthly tent was copied.' "

The Sanctuary at Shiloh

Now back in the U.S.A., I have just reviewed the scholarly evidence for the location of the tabernacle in Shiloh. Scholars generally agree that Tell Shiloh is the site of ancient Shiloh. The location fits the detailed geographical data in the biblical record: "Shiloh, which is north of Bethel, on the east side of the highway that goes up from Bethel to Shechem, and south of Lebonah" (Judges 21:19). Tell Shiloh is north of modern Beitin (probably biblical Bethel), south of the modern village Lubban Sharquya (probably biblical Lebonah), and just to the east of the modern highway from Jerusalem to Nablus (biblical Shechem; probably about the same route as the ancient road).

Shiloh was an excellent site for the sanctuary. It was near the geographical center of Palestine and thus easily accessible to all the tribes of Israel. Archaeological surveys have shown that no one occupied the site at the time of the Israelite conquest, and that it was in an area of Canaan only sparsely populated by Canaanites.[1] Joshua had thoroughly conquered and dispossessed this part of the land so pilgrims coming to the sanctuary would be safe. Field tests have shown that the acoustics and visual capacity at Shiloh made it an ideal spot for a large assembly to hear and see the worship proceedings.[2] At the same time, steep slopes surround the tell on all sides except the south, providing for excellent defense from enemy attack.

There remains some scholarly debate over the precise location of the tabernacle at Shiloh, with proponents of a site on the summit to the south or to the north of the tell.[3] Those suggesting the summit of the tell fail to recognize that the top simply has no level space of sufficient size to contain the tabernacle enclosure.[4]

Against those who suggest an area south of the tell,[4] a close reading of the biblical passage in 1 Samuel 4:12-14 seems to indicate that the sanctuary was north of the city itself, not south. After the battle of Ebenezer, in which the Philistines took the ark, the Israelites sent a messenger back to Shiloh. He first passed through the town, with its only entrance being to the south, and then came and told Eli, thus implying that the sanctuary compound was just north of the city.[5]

Asher Kaufman has given the most thorough examination of this question and offers weighty arguments to support the northern location on the tell.[6] While in Israel I had the privilege of interviewing Professor Kaufman at his home and also of visiting Tell Shiloh myself, as indicated in my journal entry earlier. I am personally persuaded that the weight of evidence favors the flat, artificially created rock terrace on the northern edge of the tell, some 50 feet lower in elevation than the summit.

This location is just the right size to fit the dimensions mentioned in Scripture for the sanctuary—I stepped it off myself to make sure! It is the only place on the tell with a level area big enough to hold the sanctuary precincts. In fact, such a level area on the side of a tell, with the rest of the mound rough and uneven, is unique among the many tells in Israel that I have visited.

Archaeological excavations have uncovered storerooms adjoining the northern edge of the tell, with numerous large stone jars, silos with huge quantities of carbonized wheat, and various sanctuary-related objects—all burned in a fierce conflagration, probably when the Philistines destroyed Shiloh about 1050 B.C. A deposit of earth, ashes, and stones some five feet thick, dating from the time of Joshua and the later judges, occurs in the northeast corner of the tell, near where the door of the sanctuary precincts would have been. In the debris of this deposit archaeologists found a large quantity of broken pottery (shallow bowls, juglets, lamps, chalices, and cooking pots) and animal bones, probably buried after serving their function as sacred vessels and sacrificial animals in the sanctuary services. From all the available evidence, it seems clear that Tell Shiloh, and probably the flat terrace on the northern part of the tell, was the site of Israel's sanctuary.

The Sanctuary in Joshua

Why have I devoted so much space to discussing the location of the sanctuary at Shiloh? Because the sanctuary and its services form the heart of the book of Joshua! As we noted in the introduction, the literary structure of Joshua highlights the centrality of the sanctuary. At the apex of the first half of the book lies the building of a sacrificial altar at Shechem. And at the very center of the second half of the book comes the erecting of the tabernacle at Shiloh.

For a book ostensibly about wars of conquest and dividing of inheritance, it is amazing how many stories in Joshua highlight the sanctuary and items related to its services. The book opens with the Lord telling Joshua to meditate day and night upon the five books of Moses—which contain some 50 chapters devoted totally to describing the sanctuary and its services! When Israel crosses the Jordan River, the focus of the people and the story centers upon the ark—the sacred article of furniture in the Most Holy Place of the sanctuary. Immediately afterward, Israel observes the Passover—one of three festivals in which all the people were to come to the sanctuary. In the taking of Jericho, the "weapons of war" were items from the sanctuary—again the ark of the covenant carried by the priests, and also the shofar, the ram's horn trumpet that was the "calling" instrument of the sanctuary.

As we have already pointed out, after the victory at Ai came the covenant renewal ceremony at Shechem. At this ceremony we find the ark in the center stage, the sacrificial altar built upon Mount Ebal, and the writing and reading of the book of the law—stored by the ark in the sanctuary Holy of Holies. The Gibeonite narrative ends with the Gibeonites becoming water carriers and woodcutters—for the services of the sanctuary!

And now, as the centerpiece for the second half of the book, Israel erects the sanctuary at Shiloh, and Joshua and the high priests draw lots for the division of Israel's inheritance at its door.

The sanctuary focus continues into the later parts of the book. We find descriptions of the cities of refuge and other Levitical cities, rich with typological sanctuary allusions (see *Patriarchs and Prophets*, pp. 515-517). After all the tribes of Israel had received their inheritance and the two and a half tribes had returned across the Jordan, a major source of misunderstanding and potential conflict concerned the sanctuary: the building of a rival altar east of the Jordan seemed to imply that the two and a half tribes were focusing their attention elsewhere than the one true sanctuary.

Finally, the last scene of the book, recorded in Joshua 24, returns to Shechem and another covenant renewal ceremony. A scribe recorded the words of the covenant "in the Book of the Law of God," which was deposited beside the ark, and a stone of remembrance was set up "under the oak that was by the sanctuary of the Lord" (verse 26). Apparently the priests brought the sanctuary temporarily to Shechem from Shiloh for this final public ceremony of Joshua's life.[7]

Thus references to the sanctuary fill the book of Joshua! And each sanctuary scene has its typological messages to give to us, spiritual Israel, gathered around the heavenly sanctuary. I invite you to review the book of Joshua with the sanctuary scenes in mind, and meditate upon their typological significance, based upon the principles outlined in chapter 2 of this book. I am convinced that if our battles of spiritual conquest and possessing of our spiritual inheritance were centered in, and suffused with, the sanctuary message and experience, we would find God working mightily and miraculously for us as for Israel of old! Eyes on the heavenly sanctuary, spiritual Israel!

Joshua's Inheritance

Even Joshua's choice of his personal inheritance probably has a connection with his focus upon and attraction to the sanctuary. "Thursday, May 19. Here I stand on the remote and little-visited site of Tell Tibneh. The tell is not even listed on my regular archaeological map—I had to pore over detailed topographical survey maps written in modern Hebrew to find its location. The narrow sixth-level secondary road (the narrowest kind of paved road in Israel, width less than five meters) wound its way from the western plain up through the Shephelah (foothills) into the mountains of Ephraim. We passed olive groves on the steep terraced mountainsides and down in the deep valleys, where patient, back-breaking removal of millions of large stones had exposed fertile soil and produced endless rock-piled walls among the trees. Virtually no visitors come on this road because it is in the occupied West Bank, in a very potentially volatile area where remote, strongly fortified, and heavily armed Israeli settlements intrude upon the life of the mountain Arab villages.

"I inquired at the guarded entrance of one of the Israeli settlements as to the whereabouts of Tell Tibneh. Though it turned out we were very near the site, the settlers we talked to knew nothing of its existence. But they were clear about one thing—we should not be in the area unless we had guns to defend ourselves. They warned, 'Do not drive off the main highway onto any back road or into any Arab village, or you will never come back. You'll have 200 Arabs surround you and do you in.' We thanked them for the advice, got back in the VW minivan, and continued to follow the lead of our topographical map. Finally we spotted the tell, an artificial mound rising almost unnoticeably beside the road, and I scrambled up through the brush to the summit. . . .

"And so now I finally stand on Tell Tibneh, the site in the footsteps of Joshua that I have wanted to visit while in Israel this time perhaps more than any other, but never thought I would get a chance. Tell Tibneh—ancient Timnath Serah, the inheritance of Joshua!

"Timnath Serah means 'the portion that remains,' and I recall the biblical record of how Joshua waited until after all of Israel had received their inheritance, and then he took what remained. He chose no extensive and prominent territory, but rather a small, remote site in the rugged mountains of Ephraim. A backwoods mountain town for the general and head of state of Israel!

"The tell is not large. I step off about 300 yards by 100 yards. Joshua built a modest-sized village. It all fits with the unselfish spirit and noble character of Joshua that emerges from the biblical account. What a testimony of servant leadership for today's church officers and public officials!

"Crisscrossing the tell, I look at the cisterns, the remains of buildings, and the fragments of pottery. In every direction from the summit of the tell I have a commanding view of the terraced and rocky-ledged mountains of Ephraim. Gazing down the steep slope of the deep ravine at the northern edge of the tell, I see an Arab shepherd boy watching his flock of goats. When I wave at him, he waves back, then calls out in broken English, 'Danger! Maybe forbidden by the [Israeli] soldiers for you to be there! You should ask their permission!' What a tragedy—the Arabs were obviously as afraid of the Israelis as the Israelis were of them!

"I wonder, *Why did Joshua choose this particular small town in Israel?* Then I look to the east, and with my eye follow the road as it winds through the mountains. And I remember that almost straight east, about 12 miles as the crow flies, a little more through the wadis or on the crooked mountain road, lies Tell Shiloh! Joshua, who (as we discussed above) centered his ministry in the sanctuary service, retired to a country setting that is only a day's journey from the tabernacle of the Lord. Even in his sunset years he gives testimony to the importance of the sanctuary in his life!"

Finally Joshua could rest in the land of his inheritance. In fact, God had now given all Israel settled rest and repose in the land of promise. "The Lord gave them rest *[nûaḥ* all around, according to all that He had sworn to their fathers. . . . Not a word failed of any good thing which the Lord had spoken to the house of Israel. All came to pass" (Joshua 21:44, 45).

God longs to give us the same exhilarating fulfillment of the promises of spiritual rest and inheritance in spiritual Canaan (see Heb. 4:1-11). Shall we claim His unfailing promises today?

---

[1] See Israel Finkelstein, "Shiloh Yields Some, but Not All, of Its Secrets: Location of Tabernacle Still Uncertain," *Biblical Archaeology Review,* January/February 1986, p. 40.

[2] See B. Cobbey Crisler, "The Acoustics and Crowd Capacity of Natural Amphitheaters in Palestine," *Biblical Archaeologist* 39, No. 4 (1976): 130-134.

[3] Finkelstein, p. 41.

[4] Michael Avi-Yonah, in *Encyclopedia Judaica* (Jerusalem: Keter, 1971), vol. 14, col. 1402.

[5] For further elaboration, see Asher S. Kaufman, "Fixing the Site of the Tabernacle at Shiloh," *Biblical Archaeology Review,* November/December 1988, pp. 49, 52.

[6] Kaufman, pp. 46-52. Kaufman adds further confirming evidence to support the same location suggested more than 100 years ago by Charles W. Wilson of the Palestine Exploration Fund in London. Kaufman (p. 52) counters Finkelstein's argument against the location on the northern part of the tell, which he based upon lack of building remains and pottery there from the period of Joshua and the Judges, by citing Finkelstein's own earlier comment that because "all construction in all periods attempts to lay building foundations directly on bedrock, the building activity of later periods . . . caused extensive damage to earlier strata. Older buildings had often been destroyed and sometimes even eradicated" (citing Finkelstein, p. 26). We might add that according to the biblical record there was no "building" there in the first place, but rather the *tent* of meeting, which would not have left architectural remains when burned or removed. Any broken pottery in the sacred enclosure would have been carefully removed and deposited in a dump or burial—the evidence for which Finkelstein found in abundance at the northeast edge of the tell!

[7] Madvig ("Joshua," pp. 365, 370) cogently argues for this position. But even if some location at Shechem was designated the *miqdaš* ("sanctuary, holy place"), it would still highlight the sanctuary motif.

Passing
the Torch

12

In the last three chapters of the book of Joshua we hear the old general of Israel delivering three farewell speeches. Joshua 22 brings us back full cycle. At the beginning of the book he charges the two and a half tribes to join with their fellow Israelites in the conquest of Canaan (Joshua 1:12-18), and now Joshua addresses these Transjordanian tribes as they are ready to return across the Jordan and rejoin their families. In the literary structure of Joshua, chapter 22 also matches the summary of the inheritance for the two and a half tribes at the end of the first half of the book (Joshua 12:1-6).

Blessing the Eastern Tribes

Joshua commends the tribes of Reuben and Gad and the half of the tribe of Manasseh for their faithfulness in doing their duty in not forsaking their kinspeople till the wars of conquest west of the Jordan were completed. They deserve his accolades. Imagine leaving family and friends behind for some seven years to go to the assistance of your countrymen. I was away from my wife only two months during my most recent trip to the Middle East, and we both thought we would die! The experience made me determine never to leave my wife and daughter alone again for that long a time—and we had E-mail and fax and telephone and airmail and the courier service of other travelers to keep in touch with. Perhaps some of the two and a half tribes did get some rest and relaxation across the Jordan between campaigns, but they still need to be commended for their loyalty to the welfare of the unified nation of Israel.

But their return to the territory of Transjordan did have its dan-ger—danger of peacetime stagnation and forgetfulness of the Lord in their isolated location across the Jordan. Joshua has commended their previous covenant loyalty. Now in a single sentence pregnant with meaning he summarizes the whole inspired counsel of Moses in Deuteronomy: "But take diligent heed to do the commandment and the law which Moses the servant of the Lord commanded you, to love the Lord your God, to walk in all His ways, to keep His commandments, to hold fast to Him, and to serve Him with all your heart and with all your soul" (Joshua 22:5).

Moses gave similar appeals in his farewell sermon before his death (see Deut. 4:4, 29; 6:5; 10:12, 13). Here is one of the great scriptural summaries of the covenant relationship God longs for us to maintain with Him. It includes the outward conformity to the commandments of the Torah, the intimate covenant attachment (Hebrew *dābaq*, "cleave" or "cling," as Adam and Eve did in Gen. 2:24) to Yahweh and ardent affection for Him. As the patriarchs had done for their posterity, Joshua blesses the two and a half tribes, sending them home heavy with the plunder from war.

Misunderstanding

One expects an uneventful return of the two and a half tribes to their Transjordanian homes, but an incident occurs before they get beyond the Jordan River—an incident of real-life circum-stances that provides us with potent principles of human relations. One is pressed to find a more instructive story in teaching how (and how not) to deal with the kind of interpersonal misunder-standings that develop in the home, church, and society.

The two and a half tribes built an altar at the Jordan that the nine and a half interpreted as an act of treachery against the Lord. Who was at fault in the misunderstanding? Both parties!

"The two and a half tribes had been at fault in entering, with-out explanation, upon an act open to such grave suspicions. . . . The ten tribes remembered how, in Achan's case, God had re-buked the lack of vigilance to discover the sins existing among them. Now they resolved to act promptly and earnestly; but in seeking to shun their first error, they had gone to the opposite extreme. Instead of making courteous inquiry to learn the facts in the case, they had met their brethren with censure and condemnation" (*Patriarchs and Prophets*, pp. 518, 519).

The same problems exist today, and the same principles of human relations that we can derive from this story will stand us in good stead. I recently had a misunderstanding with a very good friend, and it caused us both months of untold grief and anguish. If we had only been open in explaining the actions we were contemplating or taking, and the reasons for them—as the two and a half tribes should have done—what pain we could have avoided! If we had only made "courteous inquiry" to learn the facts, without censure or condemnation, how speedily we could have resolved the problem!

How much our churches need to have a "spirit of kindness, a courteous, forbearing deportment" in dealing with the erring (*ibid.,* p. 520). "Happy will it be for God's people when they shall be able to unite zeal and firmness with meekness and forbearance" (Ellen G. White, in *Signs of the Times*, May 12, 1881).

The response of the two and a half tribes to the false accusations made against them teaches us still another important principle:

"The wisdom displayed by the Reubenites and their companions is worthy of imitation. While honestly seeking to promote the cause of true religion, they were misjudged and severely censured; yet they manifested no resentment. They listened with courtesy and patience to the charges of their brethren before attempting to make their defense, and then fully explained their motives and showed their innocence. Thus the difficulty which had threatened such serious consequences was amicably settled" (*Patriarchs and Prophets*, p. 520).

Here we find practical principles for those falsely accused today: listening courteously and patiently, followed by a calm and complete explanation of actions and motivations. Shall we imitate the two and a half tribes in our conflict resolution?

When we are misunderstood and falsely accused, it is tempting to act prematurely and in anger. But God's way is so much better, and His promise of conflict resolution is sure:

"Even under false accusation those who are in the right can afford to be calm and considerate. God is acquainted with all that is misunderstood and misinterpreted by men, and we can safely leave our case in His hands. He will as surely vindicate the cause of those who put their trust in Him as He searched out the guilt of Achan. Those who are actuated by the spirit of Christ will possess that charity which suffers long and is kind" *(ibid.).*

At the same time, those who are doing the accusing, zealously opposing sin, also need to learn lessons from the response of the nine and a half tribes. They "should ever seek to take the most favorable view of their brethren, and should rejoice when they are found guiltless" *(The SDA Bible Commentary,* Ellen G. White Comments, vol. 2, p. 999).

Tucked away here at the end of the book of Joshua, we have priceless principles for conflict management and resolution that will lead to unity in our homes and churches and schools! Perhaps when we have resolved specific conflicts, we might creatively designate tangible monuments to our unity and solidarity, as the replica altar became at the Jordan. We can point our children and new members of our church to how by God's grace conflict gave way to unity without the sacrifice of principle.

Passing the Torch

We now pass in the flow of history to "a long time after the Lord had given rest to Israel." It is probably some 20 to 25 years later, when Joshua was old and advanced in age. He calls for all Israel, apparently represented by their heads, their judges, and their officers.

This speech, recorded in Joshua 23, is not, like the previous chapter, merely a farewell to those returning to their inheritances. It is the last words of Israel's aged captain as he passes the torch to a new generation of leaders. Like Joseph in his deathbed message to his brothers (Gen. 50:24, 25), Moses in his farewell song and blessing (Deut. 31; 32), and Paul's farewell to the Ephesian elders (Acts 20:25-29, 31), so Joshua gives his final charge to his successors in leadership.

The deathbed message of a great man often contains profound wisdom, and Joshua's farewell speech, coming under divine inspiration, has a timeless message for both ancient and spiritual Israel. Where can you find a more wonderful promise of victory than that given in Joshua 23:10: "One man of you shall chase a thousand, for the Lord your God is He who fights for you, as He has promised you"?

Or where can you find a more noble charge than that in verse 6 as Joshua harkens back to the charge God gave him in the beginning of the book: "Therefore be very courageous to keep and to do all that is written in the Book of the Law of Moses, lest you turn aside from it to the right hand or to the left"? Joshua uses two intimate expressions that poignantly depict the deep personal relationship that he longed for them to have with the Lord. "Hold fast [dābaq, 'cling'] to the Lord your God" (verse 8). And again, "Therefore take diligent heed to yourselves, that you love the Lord your God" (verse 11). The great evangelical preacher Alan Redpath wrote, " 'Take heed to love.' If I could choose the subject for the last sermon I ever preached, this would be my text."*

Where else can you find stronger warnings against apostasy (verse 7) and association and intermarriage with idolaters (verse 12)? Joshua couples them with vivid depictions of the dire consequences of disobedience. He tells Israel's leaders that idolatrous associations and alliances would become "snares and traps to you, and scourges on your sides and thorns in your eyes, until you perish from this good land which the Lord your God has given you" (verse 13).

Then Joshua concludes with the most solemn reminders of God's faithfulness to the covenant—to both the blessings and the curses! He uses memories of God's signal blessings in Israel's conquest of Canaan as a stunning indicator of the surety of God's covenant curses upon them should they transgress the covenant and turn away from God to idolatry. Thus he underscores both the mercy and justice of the covenant God.

The farewell message of Old Testament Joshua at the end of his life finds its counterpart in the farewell message of the new Joshua to His disciples on the eve of His death. Jesus, the new Joshua, also gave precious promises to those future leaders of His church. He also presented a noble charge, utilizing terms of intimacy to describe their relationship with God. Emphasizing our need to cling to the divine Vine, He urged us to take heed to love God and one another. And He too warned of apostasy and its dire consequences.

And then the antitypical Joshua incarnated all of these points in the experience of His passion and on the cross revealed the indissoluble union between mercy and justice in the character of God.

"Justice and Mercy stood apart, in opposition to each other, separated by a wide gulf. The Lord our Redeemer clothed His divinity with humanity, and wrought out in behalf of man a character that was without spot or blemish. He planted His cross midway between heaven and earth, and made it the object of attraction which reached both ways, drawing both Justice and Mercy across the gulf. Justice moved from its exalted throne, and with all the armies of heaven approached the cross. There it saw One equal with God bearing the penalty for all injustice and sin. With perfect satisfaction Justice bowed in reverence at the cross, saying, It is enough" *(The SDA Bible Commentary,* Ellen G. White Comments, vol. 7, p. 936).

Take heed to the farewell addresses of the two Joshuas!

---

*Alan Redpath, *Victorious Christian Living: Studies in the Book of Joshua* (Old Tappan, N.J.: Fleming H. Revell, 1955), p. 238.

"We Will Serve the Lord"

13

More than a quarter century ago I first visited the modern state of Israel, just one week after the Six-Day War. Many parts of the country were still off-limits to travel because of the land mines planted there, but shortly after arriving I was able to go to Shechem. At that time I stood in the Vale of Shechem, gazed up at those mighty "shoulders" of the valley, Mount Ebal and Mount Gerizim, and thought of Joshua and Israel renewing their covenant with the Lord there at the beginning of the conquest. Now this spring, more than 25 years later, I returned to see Shechem again. I stood on Mount Gerizim and looked out over the scene of covenant renewal, and renewed my own covenant with God.

I feel like I have really walked in the footsteps of Joshua, for he too came to Shechem shortly after his arrival in Canaan, and then more than 25 years later returned to Shechem for another covenant renewal.

The Covenant-Renewal Ceremony

In the ancient Near East of Joshua's day it was common practice within international politics for the vassals (subjects) to periodically renew their covenant with their suzerain (overlord) in a public ceremony. We have a number of examples in Scripture in which Israel conducts such an oath of allegiance before its Suzerain, Yahweh. For example, the whole book of Deuteronomy closely parallels in structure the covenant-making or covenant-renewing proceedings of international covenants (or treaties), especially as illustrated in the Hittite suzerainty treaties of that time.[1]

The major elements of the covenant-renewal ceremonies of Joshua's day are present in Joshua 24. First comes the preamble, in which the suzerain identifies himself. The divine Suzerain introduces Himself, "Thus says the Lord [Yahweh] God of Israel" (verse 2). The second element is an historical prologue in which the suzerain reviews the past benefactions he has bestowed upon his vassal. In Joshua 24 Yahweh, the Suzerain, rehearses His mighty acts in the history of Israel, from the call of Abraham out of an idolatrous nation and family to the mighty deliverance at the Exodus and on to the successful conquest of Canaan (verses 2-13).

Third, there is a call for the vassal to continue to obey the covenant stipulations (commandments), to renew his undivided allegiance and covenant loyalty to the suzerain, motivated by what the suzerain has done for his vassal. Joshua, acting as Yahweh's spokesman, calls Israel to "fear the Lord, serve Him in sincerity and in truth, and put away the [foreign] gods" (verse 14), and to "choose for yourselves this day whom you will serve" (verse 15).

Fourth, such covenant treaties refer (either implicitly or explicitly) to the blessings that will accrue for obedience and the curses for disobedience. Joshua had already explicitly mentioned both the blessings and curses in his preliminary farewell address to the leaders of Israel (see Joshua 23:10-16), and here in Joshua 24 the blessings are implicit in the historical prologue, where Yahweh mentions what He is continuing to do for His covenant people (verse 13). Israel's aged leader himself emphasizes the consequences of disobedience: "If you forsake the Lord and serve foreign gods, then He will turn and do you harm and consume you, after He has done you good" (verse 20).

Fifth, you will find a listing of witnesses to the covenant renewal ceremony. Joshua calls the people themselves to be witnesses: "You are witnesses against yourselves that you have chosen the Lord for yourselves, to serve Him" (verse 22). He also set up a large stone as a witness, saying to the people, "Behold, this stone shall be a witness to us, for it has heard all the words of the Lord which He spoke to us. It shall therefore be a witness to you, lest you deny your God" (verse 27).

Finally, the parties will deposit the covenant-renewal document for future periodic reading by the vassal. "Joshua made [literally, "cut"][2] a covenant with the people that day, and made for them a statute and an ordinance in Shechem. Then Joshua wrote these words [of the covenant] in the Book of the Law of God" (verses 25, 26). As part of the "Book of the Law of God," they would be deposited in Israel's sanctuary and read every seven years (see Deut. 31:9-13).

You Are There!

Along with the commonly accepted covenant-renewal procedural steps, Yahweh includes one more element. As part of the historical prologue He underscores a powerful principle already introduced at the time of the Exodus—the principle of personalization.

When God instructed Israel about the Passover service as they were just about to leave Egypt, He stated that each succeeding generation was to say to their children, "This is done because of what the Lord did for *me* when I came up from Egypt" (Ex. 13:8). Each generation was to personalize the Exodus, to consider that they themselves came out of Egypt.

Thus 40 years later, when most of the adult generation who actually witnessed the Exodus were dead, Moses still instructed Israel to tell their children when they entered Canaan, "*We* were slaves of Pharaoh in Egypt, and the Lord brought *us* out of Egypt with a mighty hand" (Deut. 6:21). And when Moses described the covenant made with Israel at Mount Sinai, even though many in his audience had not literally been present at Sinai, Moses insisted: "The Lord did not make this covenant with our fathers [only], but with us, those who are here today, all of us who are alive" (Deut. 5:3). All were to consider that they had been there and that God had made the covenant personally with them!

Joshua 24 continues and makes more vivid than ever this principle of personalization. Even though almost all of those who literally witnessed the Exodus have already died, notice that God insists that His audience is to consider that they were there! When the Lord describes His acts of deliverance for the children of Israel, He deliberately shifts back and forth from referring to "your fathers" (those who were literally present at the Exodus) to "you" (the later generation who were to consider that they were there):

"Afterward I brought *you* out. Then I brought *your fathers* out of Egypt, and *you* came to the sea; and the Egyptians pursued *your fathers* with chariots and horsemen to the Red Sea. So *they* cried out to the Lord; and He put darkness between *you* and the Egyptians, brought the sea upon them, and covered them. And *your eyes* saw what I did in Egypt" (Joshua 24:5-7).

While the fathers of the present audience had literally experienced the Exodus, God now urges the later generation to reckon that they personally had come out of Egypt. God says in effect, *"You are there!"*

When I was a child, my parents allowed me to watch two television programs each week. One was *Lassie,* about the beloved collie dog. The other was *You Are There.* Hosted by Walter Cronkite, it would take the viewing audience to some past historical event that the cast reenacted as if we the television audience were also there. I remember being "on" the *Titanic* the night it sank, and without enough lifeboats we went down with the ship. However, just before we plunged into the icy ocean depths, the scene faded to Walter Cronkite, who intoned in his deep bass voice, "You are there!"

God also tells us when we read the events of Israel's history, "You are there!" For we are spiritual Israel (Gal. 3:29), and the principle of personalization is for us as much as for Israel of old. Many New Testament passages continue the "You are there" principle (see especially Heb. 4:3, 16; 6:19; 7:9; 10:19, 20; 12:22-24; cf. Gal. 3:16, 29; Eph. 1:20; 2:6; Rev. 15:1, 2). In fact, this principle becomes the very heart of the gospel, as we are to consider that we were "in Christ" when He died so that when He died we died also, and when He arose we arose with Him (2 Cor. 5:14, 15, 21; Rom. 6:3-6). In Christ—we were there!

This principle is dynamite in making the Bible come alive! The Bible is no longer only a history book about some faraway and long-ago people. It is not only a family album about our spiritual ancestors, our spiritual fathers (1 Cor. 10:1), our "roots." No, it is actually *our personal diary, our personal journal, our personal autobiography!*[3] Scripture is the story of what happened to *us* when *we* were Pharaoh's slaves, when *we* came out of Egypt, when *we* went through the Red Sea, when *we* conquered the

124

Amorites east of the Jordan, when *we* entered the land of Canaan, when God gave *us* the land of promise.

I enjoy watching my teenage daughter go through her journal, reading those special portions that bring back delightful memories. She loves reading and rereading what happened to her in the past—because she was there!

God shows us in Joshua 24 how the Scriptures can come alive to us like my daughter Rahel's journal does to her. I encourage you to read the books of the Bible and see yourself and your own personal history in those stories. Consider that God delivered *you* from Egyptian bondage. Relive those scenes as if they were your own. Get all the historical, geographical, chronological, and other background information that you can so that you can brush away the "amnesia" and vividly recall each detail of the events. Reenact each scene in your mind, savor the mighty power of God in delivering you in the account of the Exodus and the conquest. Relearn the lessons from your failures in the stories.

"Choose . . . This Day"

And most important, relive the great moments of decision for God. Hear afresh Joshua's call to you: "Choose for yourselves this day whom you will serve." See that brave warrior setting the example when he says, "But as for me and my house, we will serve the Lord" (Joshua 24:15). Then renew that enthusiastic response of you and the rest of Israel: "We also will serve the Lord, for He is our God" (verse 18).

Strip away the cobwebs of amnesia from your brain and recall the surprise you experienced as Joshua replied, "You cannot serve the Lord, for He is a holy God. He is a jealous God; He will not forgive your transgressions nor your sins" (verse 19). Then remember how you began to realize what he meant. It was not enough to make a brave resolution and pledge of allegiance. You needed to recognize your utter inability in yourself to obey God. You had to sense your need of a Saviour to forgive your sins and to give you power to obey. You needed to "trust wholly in the merits of the promised Saviour" *(Patriarchs and Prophets*, p. 524).

I invite you to continue to apply the *"You are there"* principle as Joshua makes the covenant with Israel. Along with them, covenant anew, "The Lord our God we will serve, and His voice we will obey" (Joshua 24:24). Recall in your "spiritual memory" how Joshua summoned you to witness to that covenant pledge, and how he set up a stone of witness to bring back to your minds the words of the Lord. Renew that response by repeating out loud the words "We are witnesses." And I encourage you to set up some tangible memorial of this covenant renewal. Perhaps you might wish to "erect" a "monument" right in this book by attaching your signature to the following pledge:

MY PLEDGE

TODAY, THIS VERY DAY,
BY THE GRACE OF GOD,
AND TRUSTING IN THE MERITS OF MY SAVIOUR, JESUS,

I CHOOSE

TO RENEW MY COVENANT WITH GOD
TO SERVE THE LORD WITHOUT RESERVATION
TO "ENTER GOD'S REST"
TO EXPERIENCE THE VICTORIOUS CHRISTIAN LIFE
TO POSSESS MY SPIRITUAL INHERITANCE IN CHRIST.

_____
MY SIGNATURE OF COVENANT RENEWAL

_____
DATE

"It Is Finished"

"From the top of Tell Tibneh, ancient Timnath Serah, the inheritance of Joshua, I look across the valley toward the adjoining hill to the southeast. There on the hillside is a cave, said by the local Arab villagers to be the tomb of Joshua. The biblical record says that Joshua was buried 'within the border of his inheritance at Timnath Serah' (Joshua 24:30), but we have no proof that this is the actual cave. Whether or not it is the authentic burial site of Joshua, like the stone set up at Shechem, it is a witness to us. A witness to a great man, Joshua, of whom inspiration could record, 'No stain rested upon the holy character of Joshua. . . . His life was wholly devoted to God' *(Spiritual Gifts,* vol. 4, part 1, p. 64).

"The tomb on the hillside at Timnath Serah also witnesses to another great Man, the second Joshua. Like this tomb, His tomb is empty. We don't know what happened to the bones of Old Testament Joshua, but the tomb of the new Joshua is empty because Joshua-Jesus has risen. He's alive! He's gone to heavenly Canaan, and soon He's coming back to take us to the Promised Land!"

Reader, friend, fellow pilgrim "in the footsteps of Joshua," can we make an appointment to meet together in the heavenly Canaan? To have table fellowship with Joshua and with the new Joshua! To receive our eternal inheritance in earthly Canaan made new! To enter for eternity into God's rest!

---

[1] The Hittite suzerainty treaties were first studied in detail by Victor Korošec, *Hethitische Staatsverträge* (1931); George Mendenhall was the first to compare the elements of the Hittite treaties with biblical parallels in the Decalogue, in "Covenant Forms in Israelite Tradition," *Biblical Archaeologist* (1954): 27-46, 49-76; and *Law and Covenant in Israel and the Ancient Near East* (Pittsburgh, 1955). For further discussion of the covenant structure of Deuteronomy, see Meridith Kline, *Treaty of the Great King: The Covenant Structure of Deuteronomy* (Grand Rapids, Mich.: Eerdmans, 1963, 1983), and Peter Craige, *The New International Commentary of the Old Testament: Deuteronomy* (Grand Rapids: Eerdmans, 1976), pp. 36-45. It should be pointed out that while the biblical covenant-renewal ceremonies generally follow the commonly accepted pattern of such ceremonies in international politics, they have unique elements as well. The primary uniqueness to be noted is that nowhere else in the ancient Near East do we have any example of a deity entering into a covenant with a people. In contrast to the capricious gods of the idolatrous nations surrounding Israel, only Yahweh, the faithful covenant God, binds Himself by covenant to His people.

[2] The expression "cut a covenant" derives from the common practice in the covenant ceremony of cutting the sacrificial animal in two pieces and the vassal walking between the pieces, saying in effect, "May this dismemberment be done to me if I am not faithful to the covenant." See Jeremiah 34:18-20 for a biblical example of this practice. Genesis 15 records a similar situation, except that along with the implied act of the vassal (Abram) passing between the pieces, something unheard of in ancient Near Eastern practice happens! The smoking pot and burning torch, symbolic of Yahweh Himself, pass through the pieces. Thus the Suzerain Himself is saying, May I, God, be killed if I do not remain faithful to My covenant! And ultimately we find that Yahweh does that—He dies, not for His own unfaithfulness to the covenant, but as a substitute dying for *our* unfaithfulness! What covenant love! It is possible, though not explicitly stated, that Joshua offered a sacrifice as part of the "cutting" of the covenant.

[3] Paul D. Hanson, *The People Called: The Growth of Community in the Bible* (San Francisco: Harper and Row, 1986), p. 537; although coming to Scripture with critical presuppositions, Hanson nonetheless recognizes the "you are there" principle and indicates that the Bible "is in effect our spiritual autobiography as people drawn to the living God."